Praise for *Imperfect Spirituality*

"The humorous and candid narrative in this book delivers lighthearted yet significant direction for integrating traditional spiritual techniques with the imperfections that characterize daily life....Practical tips for turning ordinary moments into opportunities for spiritual growth, many of which can be squeezed in while brushing your teeth or waiting for the bus, punctuate this clear and affable spiritual guide for the rest of us."

—*Publishers Weekly*

"*Imperfect Spirituality* presumes you know your relationship to the Divine and shines light on your relationship with Yourself. Polly hooked me at 'Don't put any more raisins up your nose.' While Campbell references a buffet of respected sources, the path is her own. It's funny, functional guidance in the accessible voice of a good friend. Read from start to finish, or open anywhere for a dip. Her words reach out...and touch your heart."

—Mary Anne Radmacher, author of *Live Boldly*

"Polly Campbell's *Imperfect Spirituality* is a welcome addition to the field of self-help and spiritual living. Her book is, above all, practical. No lofty, from-the-mountaintop sermonizing here—this is a woman who found an opportunity for spiritual practice while dealing with a raisin up her child's nose! As Polly reminds us, our ability to connect with the Divine is always possible, and in everyday occurrences, and her book is full of helpful stories, reflections, and exercises for doing exactly that. There may be no such thing as perfection, in spirituality or anything else, but Polly Campbell has given us a truly wonderful resource for living our lives with more connection, compassion, and calm."

—Maggie Oman Shannon, editor of *Prayers for Healing*

"Congratulations to Polly Campbell for keeping it real! Her honest, frank, and often hilarious view of the challenges we create when we try to run from who we are is very empowering. You're sure to laugh along the way as author Polly Campbell shares her own insights, stresses, and stories en route to a more authentic life."

—Dr. Judith Wright, author of *The Soft Addiction Solution*

"*Imperfect Spirituality* is a beautiful, inspiring journey to self-acceptance through the lens of spirituality. Campbell quiets the mind and feeds the soul so you can powerfully embrace who and how you are and liberate yourself from standards that actually limit rather than inspire you. When Campbell guides us in embracing our imperfection, what she is most telling us is to relish our extraordinary uniqueness. This luminous work will leave you resolved and new."

—Rosie Molinary, author of
Beautiful You: A Daily Guide to Radical Self-Acceptance

"Is there a more perfect word for spirituality than imperfect? I think not. Perfection is hoisted as the great and mighty goal, but none of us (aside from a few mystics and saints) are there yet. Thanks to Polly Campbell for this delicious treatise on the totally perfect state of imperfection. We can be at peace with where we are—in our lives, in our messes, in our moments. And guess what? That's where perfection lies. Bless you, Polly, for showing us the crooked road."

—Janet Conner, author of *Writing Down Your Soul*

"In *Imperfect Spirituality* Polly Campbell reminds us that the path to enlightenment begins exactly where you are right now. Every moment of our lives is a sacred opportunity to be present and to deepen and expand our capacity to give and receive love. Open this book to any page and allow the stories and practical tips to illuminate your path to enlightenment."

—Susyn Reeve, author of *The Inspired Life*

imperfect spirituality

imperfect spirituality

extraordinary enlightenment for ordinary people

polly campbell

foreword by nina lesowitz

Published in the United States by Viva Editions, an imprint of Cleis Press, Inc., 2246 Sixth Street, Berkeley, California 94710.

Printed in the United States.
Cover design: Scott Idleman/Blink
Cover photograph: Fotosearch
Text design: Frank Wiedemann
First Edition.
10 9 8 7 6 5 4 3 2 1

Trade paper ISBN: 978-1-936740-18-5
E-book ISBN: 978-1-936740-27-7

Library of Congress Cataloging-in-Publication Data

Campbell, Polly L.
 Imperfect spirituality : extraordinary enlightenment for ordinary people / by Polly Campbell. -- 1st ed.
    p. cm.
 ISBN 978-1-936740-18-5 (pbk. : alk. paper)
1. Self-actualization (Psychology) 2. Mind and body. I. Title.
BF637.S4C342 2012
204--dc23
                                        2012026199

For Jerry,
Your coffee and kindness kept me going at all hours. Thanks
for knowing all that I am and loving me anyway.

For Piper,
So wise and strong and creative. I learn so much from you
and love you more than the moon, Ladybug.

You build on failure. You use it as a stepping-stone. Close the door on the past. You don't try to forget the mistakes but you don't dwell on it. You don't let it have any of your energy, or any of your time, or any of your space.

—JOHNNY CASH

ACKNOWLEDGMENTS

Writing a book—like creating a spiritual life—requires faith, patience, persistence, and a whole bunch of people in your life who are smarter and more fun than you are. Though writing is usually done alone, producing a book is a group effort, and I had a fantastic group behind me.

These people kept me going with their love and support; their good ideas and funny jokes; their willingness to babysit and do extra chores—all so that I could keep working.

Thank you, Jerry and Piper, for giving me space to follow my dream and for keeping the house tidied and never once complaining that I wore the same sweatpants every day. To my Mom and Dad, Lynda and Steve Campbell, thanks for teaching me to believe that I could accomplish anything and for being open to my ideas and passions long before they made sense. To Paige Campbell and my favorite boy Quinn, thanks for your love and support in everything. To my grandmother, Louise Larson, I so admire your curiosity and desire to learn. You infused me with that spirit. I'm certain your love of language and books inspired me to become a writer.

Sherri, thanks for the regular messages and pep talks, the feedback and friendship; it all made a difference. Thanks,

Acknowledgments

....

Regina, for cheering me on. I so appreciate your encouragement and enthusiasm. Thanks to the Core 4: Lori, for your "thinking-of-you" notes; Megan, for your thoughtful discussions. Thanks to Kelly Hatler, for the cake, the friendship, and the free therapy sessions. To Lewis for years of just putting up with me; and to both you and Dong for your excitement when I finally made the deal. Thanks also to Sally-Jo, for being a coach when I needed coaching and a friend when I needed friendship. Sam and Bev, thanks for your support and interest, always.

To Kelly James-Enger, whew girl, your generosity and intelligence helped me learn what I needed to know to write this puppy, and your humor just made it more fun. Thanks for the regular encouragement and friendship through all these years. Jodi Helmer, thanks for your enthusiasm for this project. I'm glad you're out there and grateful for your friendship.

So many others offered bits of encouragement and help that made both me and the book better, thanks: Jennifer Haupt, Rosie Molinary, Kate Hanley, Andrea Mather, Denise Schipani.

Thank you to agent extraordinaire, Jennifer Lawler, who took a chance on me and then offered insight at various points along the way. To Neil Salkind, from the Salkind Agency, Studio B, thanks bud, for not giving up. To the bright spirit and awesome editor Brenda Knight, marketing manager Nancy Fish, and all the folks at Viva Editions, thanks for giving a platform to these words.

I relied on the insights of so many wise people for this book. I thank them: Martha Beck, I'm a huge fan and learn from you every time I read your work. Ann Quasman, you are a difference maker; Judith Wright, your encouragement and ideas inspired me; Julie Rudiger, I value your expertise and your friendship; Donald Altman, your wise guidance and perspective have helped me connect to my work and my spirit in a new way. Thanks, too, to Terry Real, Paul Hertel, Katie Hendricks, Cynthia Pury, Ben Michaelis, Laurie Essig, Rev. Susan Sparks, Kristin Neff, Arielle Ford, Michael Steger, Steven Hayes, and Rabbi Brad Hirschfield. Rabbi, the conversation we had still resonates with me.

I am profoundly grateful to those who shared their stories, complete with their flops and failures and imperfections, so that we could all learn. Their stories are our stories. Thanks to: Richard Earls, Ann Quasman, Kelly James-Enger, Paige Campbell, Himavat Ishaya, Bonnie Matthews, Kristin and Josh Mauer, Jennifer Haupt, Brent Mather, Rhonda Sciortino, Jessica Riesenbeck, and Jason Marshall.

Finally, a long time ago, I knew I was to be a writer. That desire was cultivated by a great group of Reading and English teachers in the Seaside School District, when I was there about a million years ago: Mrs. Barbara Gray, Mrs. Barker, Ms. Mewhinney, Mrs. Peetz Alves, Mrs. Stewart, Mrs. Freeman, Mrs. Donnigan, Mr. Nordquist, Mrs. Robnett Nordquist. No matter what it seemed then, I *was* paying attention. What you taught did make a difference. Oh, and if you do find a misplaced comma, don't worry; it's not entirely your fault.

And to all of you reading this book: Thank you. I know it takes time to ponder these pages and I know, too, that time can be hard to come by. I am honored and grateful that you would spend some of what you have with this book. I sincerely hope that you find this book both fun and helpful.

To each of you, I am grateful.

TABLE OF CONTENTS

Foreword

I n trying to be perfect, self-sacrificing, and to adhere to ideas from a couple of centuries back, we are at risk of becoming a nation of overscheduled and under-joyed button pushers. I am a big fan of Polly Campbell's blog, which I view as a spiritual retreat for those moments when I need to take a break from my busy day to reflect. And we all really do need to take time out each day for soul work. It is easy in today's hurly-burly world to get caught up in chores, errands, socializing, endless workdays, and general busyness so much we forget that we even have a soul that needs nurturing. Even children are overscheduled and stressed out! And why is this? I believe it is the very Calvinist tendencies and Puritan roots Polly speaks to in *Imperfect*

Spirituality that are driving us to the brink of exhaustion and, worst of all, world-weariness. The idea of being perfect is a trap and our culture encourages us to try to meet unreasonable ideals.

I hope Polly's well-considered exhortation to escape the "perfect" trap inspires a rising chorus of readers who choose having a life filled with meaning over self-denial. Polly's advice that "the things you try to fix, change, and deny are the very things that will expand and elevate your life" can put you on the road to enlightenment, which, as it turns out, might be in your own backyard. So, you can't afford to quit your job and trek to a mountaintop in the Himalayas? Neither can I, nor anyone else I know, but I sweep the floor as a "be here now" practice. Polly folds her family's laundry as a meditation. Doing the dishes has long been my Zen. Polly reminds us that every day offers opportunities for personal growth if you just look at your life a little differently.

Moreover, Polly reminds us that the everyday is all we have. One of the biggest a-ha's for me from *Imperfect Spirituality* is this: you take away from the world when you're not truly yourself. All that is unique and special about you was designed by the Universe. So be your extraordinary ordinary self.

With deep gratitude,
Nina Lesowitz
Co-author of *Living Life as a Thank You*

The Cracked Pot

A water bearer carried two pots of water along the path from the stream to the house. One of the pots had a crack in it and only arrived half full while the other pot was perfect and always delivered a full portion of water.

The perfect pot was proud of its accomplishments. But the cracked pot was ashamed of its own imperfection and miserable that it was able to accomplish only half of what it had been made to do.

After two years of bitter failure, the cracked pot spoke to the water bearer.

"I am ashamed of myself, and sorry that I have been able to deliver only half my load. Because of my flaws and cracks I am not as valuable to you," the pot said.

The bearer said to the pot, "Did you notice that there were flowers only on your side of the path, but not on the other pot's side? That's because I have always known about your flaw, and I planted flower seeds on your side of the path. Every day while we walk back, you've watered them."

"For two years I have been able to pick these beautiful flowers to decorate the table. Without your imperfection, without you being just the way you are, there would not be this beauty to grace the house."

Introduction

Get off the bookcase," I shrieked when I saw my daughter Sweet P, five feet up, fingers and toes curled around the edges of the shelves.

"No."

"What?"

"I don't want to," she said, pretty sassy for someone who was hanging by her tiptoes.

"Get down now." I pause, waiting for compliance. But it looks like she's about to build a nest up there. "NOW," I say. "One, two, two-and-a-half..." Dang. Here we go again. "Three."

I storm to the bookshelf and grab her off.

"Get to your room. This is unacceptable behavior." She

starts to wail and tromps to her bedroom at the end of the hall as I mentally pore over her infractions:

1. Climbing furniture, bad.
2. Sassiness to Mom, bad *and* annoying.
3. Generally, freaking the same Mom out by clinging five feet in the air over a wood floor without a safety harness or other climbing supplies, so, so bad.

I take a deep breath and head to the bedroom for the post-discipline chat. She's talking quietly to her stuffed animals, when I open the door.

"Sweet P," I say, "it is not okay to..."

"Mommy, first I need to say one fing," she says.

"What?"

"Mommy, do you always love me even when I have bad behavior?"

Her eyes are boring into the cinnamon-colored bear settled in her crisscross-applesauce lap and her hands are twisting around its little paws, but, for the first time today, she is utterly silent waiting on my answer. There are days, I'll admit, when I fantasize about running out of the house (screaming), changing my identity, and moving to the tropics (shoot, I've had days where I've fantasized about working at Subway, just to get out of the house), but there is nothing I've ever loved more than the bookshelf-climbing creature that I gave birth to. In fact, I didn't know I was capable of loving anything like I love her.

"Come here," I say. She hands me the bear and then crawls under it to get into my lap. "There is nothing you could do to make me not love you," I say, "nothing. I love you completely, no matter what."

Even as I say the words to my daughter, I wonder why I don't extend myself the same compassion and kindness. Why can't I meet my own errors and imperfections with the same grace? Why, instead of forgiveness, do I mentally pummel myself for my errors? Some days I just need a hug and a do-over, but instead I've gotten good at feeling guilty. Good at berating and blaming and criticizing and condemning myself for the unending list of stupid things I do, every day. That has to change.

For the first three years of my daughter's life (she is now five), I left myself little wiggle room, little room for error. I became very uptight and very un-fun. I was putting so much energy into getting "IT" right, figuring "IT" out, and keeping "IT" together that I forgot that the "IT" was actually me, a flexible, shifting, imperfect being. I completely stifled my own personal and spiritual growth by creating a constrictive, predictable, rule-filled routine and mindset, rather than the expansive it's-all-meant-to-be attitude I'd relied on before the baby. Any imperfection became a liability, something that could hurt us rather than teach us. I tried to eradicate the flaws within me that were sure to ruin my daughter and then of course bring on the Apocalypse.

All of this was wearing me out. The hard-ass, tough-love approach I'd been taking with myself was not working. The traditional spiritual practices I'd relied upon to guide my peaceful, fun, pre-baby life—meditation, gratitude, journaling, and lots of time alone for quiet reflection—were no longer practical. Who has an hour for meditation with a baby in the bedroom? I was tired, off-balance, bored, and disappointed by the daily routine of feeding and washing and feeding and diaper-changing and feeding, and you know what I'm talking about. I even felt bad about feeling bad. After all, wasn't having a baby just such a special experience? Wasn't I just loving every minute of it? Doesn't time go so fast?

No. It was mind-numbing, isolating, interesting, exhausting, scary, messy, amazing, and bewildering.

What was wrong with me? What kind of mother was I? I should be better at this. But still I couldn't measure up to my ideal. I couldn't come close to the mothers I saw in the pages of *Parents* magazine. It was tough to face the mornings knowing that my imperfections were on full display the minute I woke up. I felt angry, insecure, unattractive, doomed, and even a little desperate.

During this confusing, muddled time I realized I was growing, against my will, perhaps, but growing just the same. My life was expanding and I was stretching within it. Each day I was bombarded by how much I didn't know. When I began to lighten up a bit, to pay attention to those limitations and imperfections and to become aware of those uncomfortable feelings and that insecurity, I realized that I was actually moving back onto my spiritual path. I was simply outgrowing the shell of what I had practiced before.

Perhaps, then, this chronic bad mood and error-prone behavior, these feelings of overwhelm, were actually an indication that I was expanding; the discomfort was caused by me rubbing up against boundaries that no longer fit. I was growing out of who I'd been and into my more authentic self. I was evolving, becoming whole. That interpretation now felt possible, hopeful even. Perhaps becoming aware and learning to live fully with all of my imperfections *and* abilities was my spiritual practice.

The notion that we should be grateful for our imperfections seems outlandish when you consider our culture. The very model of Christianity is one of "ethical monotheism," one, righteous God that prefers divine behavior. I interpreted that to mean that I had to change something, be different or better, to achieve some semblance of perfection in order to be worthy of God and able to connect to my spiritual base. I couldn't see a way through that, because what I was doing was constantly screwing up in just about every way. Then I would become angry, blaming, and self-righteous about it. So. Not. Good.

St. Ambrose writes, "Perfection is synonymous with holiness."

Clearly, my approach of repeating mistakes for days on end was a tad bit removed from the St. Ambrose bandwagon.

I pretended not to care about those pictures in the parenting magazines of ultra-creative mothers who appeared carefree, joyful even, while their kids finger-painted above the white carpet (seriously?). But I did care. I wanted to be like them—without the finger paint of course. I wanted to move more easily in the world and be that fun model of the perfect mom. For one friggin' minute I wanted to be clean, to smell good, and to not have spit-up staining my shirt.

But I did have spit-up on my shirt. It was undeniable; have you ever smelled sour milk? So, if I couldn't clean myself up, what if I just let it go? What if I just stepped fully into the chaos and mess and spontaneity and imperfection that was me and my life? The thought of it felt freeing, exciting even, and plenty scary.

I started by giving up some control. I stopped micromanaging everything (still some, but not all), stopped blaming others. I relaxed a bit. I was kinder, less nagging. I laughed more. I stopped making excuses, admitted mistakes, and became more accountable. For a while I felt vulnerable and untethered, like this whole world would fall apart and I would float into space if I didn't hold it together just right. But there was also freedom and relief when I discovered that the only way to wholeness (and maybe holiness) was to give up the push for perfection and to know and accept my imperfections.

The first of the Four Noble Truths set forth by Buddha says: "Life is dukkha." In Sanskrit, dukkha can be translated to mean "suffering, temporary, or imperfection."

In Buddhism the belief is about letting go of your ideals, letting go of the ought-to's so that you are free to step into what is. Life is suffering. Life is impermanent and therefore we tend to view it as imperfect, unsatisfactory, or as though something is wrong. When you can become present to the experience of all of life—including this impermanence and its innate imperfection—when you can accept it, you then move toward enlightenment, Buddha teaches.

I see this as giving yourself permission to experience each moment of your life, ideal or not, and in so doing these experiences actually bring you closer to your own perfection as a self-realized individual.

"Perfection," writes Rabbi Shmuley Boteach, "is an engine that actually retards human progress, because it continually tosses humans back on a sense of their own inadequacy."

When we look deeply at our struggle and imperfection, when we move through it instead of trying to avoid, deny, and hide from ourselves and our truth, we have the opportunity then to do better and to experience more of those "perfect" spiritual moments of compassion, patience, and love. We become more spiritual beings when we give ourselves the grace and space to see and accept truly where we are, and who we are. We also get the luxury to decide who we will be in the next moment. When we understand and accept that we lashed out in anger because we were hurting, we then get to decide to move closer to our true nature of compassion and reach out in love the next time.

It is only by recognizing our flaws that we can move closer to our essence, authenticity, and our interpretations of God. That is the spiritual practice.

"We have a higher self and a lower self, a finite self and an infinite self, and we need both in order to be whole," says teacher and author Debbie Ford.

The Navajo Nation has known this and practiced this imperfection for centuries. Though their blankets and rugs are startling in their complexity and beauty, each one has a flaw, a tiny imperfection; an intentional error woven in called the "Spirit Line" or "Spirit String."

Imperfection is essential to creation, believe the Navajo artisans. To make something perfect means there is a natural disharmony, no room for growth or improvement. The Navajo believe only God can create perfection, so they sabotage their own perfection as a way to foster their own growth. "The process of creation is more important than the final product," writes Harry Walters in *Woven by the Grandmothers*. The imperfections in these blankets are part of what makes them charming and beautiful to buyers.

Our imperfections, too, can add to our charm and our beauty. They are part of our own creation and growth. To know this is an expansive, authentic way to live. It feels better than trying to hide from who we are. From this perspective, your spiritual practice becomes organic and dynamic. Instead of trying to uphold the rules imposed by Krishna (banish desire because desire is the root of evil action) or the strategies of some politicians (hide, deny, and blame others for anything that makes you look bad), you need simply to start paying attention to what you *are* doing, to what's working and what's not.

I do this, sometimes, though I still make plenty of mistakes. I can be impatient, critical, ungrateful, and irritated. I don't always like my hair and I think it's totally lame that I actually have a wardrobe that consists of my good sweats and not-for-public sweats. I mean who does that? But in all these moments I'm also learning that the imperfect path will teach me and protect me and leave room for me to grow into myself and do better, if I choose, the next time. My life now seems doable, more fun, more interesting, and more meaningful.

If you do choose this path of imperfection, three things are certain: 1. You'll get lots of practice because each moment provides the possibility for uncertainty and challenge. 2. It will feel hard and downright uncomfortable sometimes. Some mistakes are illuminating and easy, others are just plain icky, and the contrast can be painful. 3. Your life will also take on an energy, a peace, a feeling of health and well-being that you can never know by denying or hiding or Photoshopping your flaws away. There is freedom in this, a depth, a divinity, a humor, and ultimately, a power.

Choosing a practice of imperfection is about using what's available in every moment to connect more deeply with yourself. When you do this, you feel better, more energized, and genuine. You become healthier, more vibrant, and, I promise, you'll laugh more. All the chaotic, confusing, and stressful moments become filled with possibility and meaning.

This book will show you how to get there. It will help you identify, accept, and appreciate your own imperfections as an integral path to your spirit. I hope it inspires and entertains you—heck, we can laugh about this stuff. Perhaps it will lighten your load a bit and give you a new way to think about your own spiritual connection and path. The things you've been trying to hide, fix, change, and deny are the very things that will expand and elevate your life. While our practices may be imperfect, our souls never are.

By uncovering and accepting who you are, you become free to make choices that align you with your spirit. That is freedom. That is the spiritual path of imperfection.

Chapter 1:

Culture of Perfection

> Imperfection clings to a person, and if they wait
> till they are brushed off entirely, they would spin
> forever on their axis, advancing nowhere.
>
> —THOMAS CARLYLE

I'm pretty sure Buddha never had to deal with a raisin up his kid's nose. But I have. Raisins up the nose and other real-life moments are routine around here in my messy, chaotic, interesting life. A life that many days feels more like a ready-made script for television than a spiritual pursuit. But the messes and mistakes, imperfections and blunders have provided the basis for probably my broadest spiritual practice yet, the practice of imperfection, the practice of living an authentic life. It began in the backseat of a Volvo.

We were just fifteen minutes into an hour-long trip and my daughter was already fussing in the back.

"My nose hurts," she said. "I want out. I wanna be done."

"Enough," I said. "We'll get there when we get there." I spoke quickly so that I could get back to telling my husband how to drive, when to slow down, where to turn.

"I got it," he said. "If I need help driving I'll let you know."

"My nose is stuffy," said the voice from the backseat.

"But you DO need help," I said.

"I want out," my daughter said.

"Me, too," said my husband.

This was so not the picture I had imagined when I first thought about marriage and kids and family vacations and happily-ever-after. Of course I knew there would be challenges, but this was just plain irritating and inconvenient and crazy-making. Clearly my path to perfection as the ideal wife and mother was veering wildly toward the cliff's edge.

I actually fell over that cliff when the mist from my daughter's sneeze hit me in the back of the neck and the raisin that had, apparently, been jammed up her nose, rocketed past my ear sticking to the windshield in front of me.

"*That*," my husband said, "was so amazing."

"Did you see my raisin go, Mommy? My nose feels better now."

"Wow," said my husband, smiling at her in the rearview mirror.

Yes. Wow, I thought. My daughter had a raisin lodged in her nose. There goes my nomination for the "Mom of the Year Award"—again.

THE CULTURE OF PERFECTION

We live in a culture where things like "Mom of the Year Awards" and other signs of perfection are revered and coveted. We celebrate success, reward beauty, and praise people who follow the rules and don't make trouble. We do not generally celebrate mothers whose kids stuff raisins up their noses. We are not hot on people who are unsuccessful, overweight, unattractive, or destitute. What we like are those people who have it together, appear to have the perfect marriage and the beautiful house, the great job, and the clean kids.

We are a culture of perfection seekers. Collectively—yes, this means you and me—we celebrate youth, money, beauty, thinness, and ambition. We like shiny things, cleanliness, good manners, winners, and we like to be right, especially with our husbands.

It's an evolution that began centuries ago when the early

colonists to New England brought their Calvinist and Protestant beliefs about predestination and work to the New World. Historically, hard work was considered a spiritual pursuit. These early settlers believed that hard work was the will of God, and their duty was to serve God through their labors. Any wealth accumulated through this work was a sign of God's favor and indicated that you were one of the chosen ones, selected by God for salvation and eternal life.

With time, though, the religious doctrines began to fall away leaving a culture deeply embedded by capitalism and the austere Protestant work ethic, but one increasingly focused on perfection and personal gain as a sign of societal status rather than God's favor. The right careers, marriages, bodies, cars, and schools became prestigious, a way of indicating intelligence, worth, power.

In the late 1970s and early '80s this modern push for all things perfect shifted into overdrive when *Dallas* and *Dynasty* replaced more family-oriented programming like *Little House on the Prairie* and *The Waltons* as the most popular shows on television. There was this global sense, says Laurie Essig, PhD, author and assistant professor of sociology at Middlebury College, that perfect would provide everything we wanted and needed.

It's a perception that is hard to shake no matter how analytical or self-aware you are thanks to a market-driven system that is constantly telling us through commercials, magazines, and media that we must do certain things just to fit in.

"We are made to feel that we need to buy more stuff and do more stuff not even to be perfect but just to be presentable," Essig says. "It's doubtful many of us will ever be able to escape all aspects of this culture."

THE MOVE TOWARD IMPERFECTION

Even as we rail against the T.V. programs, billboards, and advertisements that objectify people and Photoshop their real-world characteristics like wrinkles and blemishes and other so-called flaws away, it's hard not to buy into this practice of perfectionism just a little bit. I think of it every morning when the light catches the gray in my hair. It's part of the natural aging process, I know, but it's causing me to look older and that feels harder to take every time I see a commercial for hair color filled with gorgeous, youthful women. I could dye my hair and get a teeny bit closer to the made-for-T.V.-ideal, but going with Rocket Red hair color is not going to smooth the wrinkles or alter the aging process. What if, though, instead of coloring my hair, I acknowledged my age and gave thanks that I've been able to live this long? What if I saw the strands of gray as a sign of privilege rather than a flaw? Then the so-called imperfections of getting older would make me feel better and they could actually become pathways to spiritual development.

I'm not saying to give up on self-improvement altogether. There's nothing wrong with a little hair dye or trying a technique to help you live well. Most of us do want to look better and feel better in our skin. We want to be better people. Personal development is valid and worthwhile when it comes from a place of curiosity and passion, when it comes from a desire to grow and to create meaning-filled lives. But too often we want to sweep away our flaws in order to measure up to some Hollywood ideal.

We invest time and put our attention on fixing, changing, avoiding, denying, and hiding our imperfections to match some contrived cultural expectation, rather than living from what's right and true for us. Let's do it differently. It's time to shift our focus and energy from what's wrong with us to what is right within us.

IN THE MOMENT PRACTICE: YOU CAN WORK WITH THIS

Take five minutes, wherever you are, and think about all the mistakes and imperfections that have actually yielded a happy or fortuitous result. Smile then, and say this out loud:

I will live this life just how it is. I will love it and have fun with it and learn from it. I am authentic and I can use all of this stuff: the messiness and confusion and ugliness and busyness and pain and joy and peace and beauty and humor and uncertainty to grow and live my best life. I will use all that I am—the greatness and the imperfections—to step into my full potential. To live my purpose. To contribute to others. To be the difference in the world. Who I am is enough.

THE LIMITS OF PERFECTION

In our quest to be the best we dye our hair, cream the wrinkles, cover the blemishes, fix the nose, and become masters at avoiding accountability. It's become easy to blame our mothers, partners, therapists, McDonald's, and the media for our troubles instead of admitting our mistakes. Here is a shocker, people:

We are fat because we ate the hamburgers, not because somebody cooked them for us.

But we don't admit to it. We don't want to fess up to our flaws or showcase our imperfections because we believe that to be wrong is to be weak. People who pursue this road to perfection tend to be more likely to cover up their errors than take responsibility for them, according to research from experts, like Gordon Flett, of York University.

This is a narrow, limiting way to live. To constantly push for perfection is to strive for an illusion. In the end there is nothing left but a whole lot of stress, insecurity, anxiety, and fear. People who pursue this route are also at higher risk for social alienation, divorce, suicide, burnout, depression, and a slate of health problems, according to research. As long as we stay this course of denying and excusing our flaws rather than recognizing, accepting, and using them to create more fabulous lives, we will remain stuck, stressed out, and disconnected from spirit.

THE POWER OF IMPERFECTION

The Japanese philosophy wabi-sabi urges us to make peace with those things that are rough or irregular; the things that don't go our way, by acknowledging that all of life is impermanent, imperfect, and incomplete—including us. Wabi-sabi finds beauty in simplicity. It appreciates the essence and authenticity of all things, even when they are apparently flawed. It is accepting of nature and life, as well as decay and death, because each one is a cycle of growth.

In ancient times appreciating imperfection was considered by some as the first step toward enlightenment. Viewing your own imperfections, with respect and awe and appreciation, will elevate your life in a way that feels more real and resonant.

Living authentically with imperfection allows you to:

Ask for help. When we worry about our failings, we don't ask for help for fear we will be found out. We don't acknowledge that we have a drinking problem, or that our business is failing. We don't access the people and things we need to survive the turmoil of our lives. When we recognize that setbacks aren't shortcomings, we are more apt to get the help we need to move through them.

Take creative risks. Imperfection and failure are inherent to innovation. When you release the need to get it right the first time, you step into your creative power.

Love completely. When you settle into a comfort zone with your imperfections you are more open and secure and able to give and receive love. It's a powerful thing to share all that you are and be loved anyhow.

Live with vitality. To frequently focus your energy and attention on trying to fix or hide what isn't working is exhausting. It depletes the energy you have to explore your talents, create new things, and indulge in healthy behaviors like exercise or learning. When you identify and make peace with your imperfections, you are free to shift your energies to your passions, talents, and purpose.

Make healthy choices. It's stressful to hide or deny aspects of your true self and that stress makes us prone to headaches, colds, and digestive troubles. It also contributes to most major, super-scary illnesses like cancer and heart disease. When you live honestly and free yourself up to fail, you'll experience big-time relief and greater health and well-being.

The practice of imperfection requires us to live from a place of personal integrity. It requires us to not only take a clear look at our imperfections, but to welcome them in with love and humor and patience and kindness, like we would the drunk aunt that shows up on Thanksgiving. Sure, it's gonna feel uncomfortable at times, but it's also freeing. It is the route to compassion and peace and tolerance and patience. It is the route to joy.

> ## POWER UP:
> Our human failings and flaws are unavoidable, but they can become sources of power and inspiration when we decide to acknowledge them and use their insights to launch the lives we desire and deserve.

THE EGO AND IMPERFECTION

Moving into the practice of imperfection is tough in the beginning. There is hell to pay when your Ego finds out you're going to shift your self-image and embrace the (gasp!) bad hair days and grouchy moments and let go of the relentless drive to measure up to the movie stars.

The practice of imperfection is a new, broader, more compassionate way of living and like anything else that is new, you've got to break it in and get used to it. I was pushed into this process when my usual (and rigid) approach to spirituality no longer left room for the big life changes that came with a new baby, job transition, and cancer scare.

When we stick to a narrow path and the perspective that there is only one right way of doing things, we miss out on the wisdom and opportunities we need and crave to grow and live a purposeful life. We get tied up in this weird mind/body/spirit disconnect where we know that perfection is unachievable, yet we still fight to obtain it. Even when we come close and have some measure of external success—we get the job, or lose the weight, or marry the quarterback—we don't enjoy it much, because we feel deep inside that we're not worthy of all this. We worry that we will be exposed for all our imperfections; that we'll slip again, gain the weight back, or end up in divorce.

That disparity between what we feel and what we do

causes some real stress and it moves us away from our core energy and essence and leaves us feeling scared and inauthentic.

IMPOSTOR SYNDROME AND IMPERFECTION

This is part of what psychologists Pauline Clance and Suzanne Imes coined the "Impostor Syndrome" back in the 1978. When you have a hard time believing in your competence or accomplishments, or you feel as though you don't deserve the success you have earned, when you feel like a fraud, you are suffering from Impostor Syndrome.

Rooted in perfectionism, Impostor Syndrome makes it hard to cope with rejection, constructive criticism, or even success. This keeps you from taking on new challenges or opportunities, because you fear you'll be unable to handle them. It is a stifling way to live.

PROCRASTINATION AND PERFECTION

When perfect is the ultimate or the only goal we are less likely to do the things that help us to grow and evolve. We are less likely to create, explore, attempt, and connect. We delay and avoid anything that may put our imperfections on display, anything that includes some risk of failure.

Joseph Ferrari, PhD, calls this "avoider procrastination." When you are embedded with a fear of failure (or even success) and deeply concerned with what others think, you rarely take on anything but the simplest tasks and seldom get anything meaningful done. An avoider procrastinator would prefer to be considered a person who lacks effort rather than one who lacks ability. But avoiding action is a sure way to limit your life.

THE PRACTICE OF IMPERFECTION

To live a big life, one that acknowledges both the garbage and greatness that make you who you are, allows you to uncover your authentic self. It doesn't require you to change or fix anything; it requires you to live fully with who you already are.

When you can do that, something interesting happens—those big flaws, the ones you stew about, aren't such a big deal anymore. You are now in a position to take an honest look at all the good and bad and see, with self-compassion and gentle criticism, what is working and what is not. Then the things you've been trying to fix and hide and change become qualities to help you launch your best life.

"Problems are the basis for all good, creative ideas," says author, life coach, and all-around wise woman, Martha Beck.

Here's how it works: You've spent two years at work trying to avoid public presentations. Instead of acknowledging that you aren't good at conveying your ideas to a group, you delegated the presentations to others. But you lived with fear, knowing that one day you'd be forced to present. Your fears and lack of speaking skills kept you trapped. You refused to apply for that management job everyone thought you'd be perfect for because you were afraid of being found out. When you finally did take an honest look at your failings, you discovered why you stink at public speaking. Instead of hiding from that knowledge, you decided to live with it and come clean with your boss. She wants to help and pays for the training you need to become a better speaker. Now the fear is gone from your life, you've learned new skills, and job opportunities have opened up. You have become an optimalist.

BECOMING AN OPTIMALIST

Optimalists, once called positive perfectionists, tend to be rooted in reality. "They are able to accept failure and emotional discomfort, as well as any positive outcomes, because optimalists know that failures present plenty of opportunity," according to happiness expert Tal Ben-Shahar, PhD.

THE PERKS OF IMPERFECTION

What we want and what our spirit needs, is to be whole and harmonious, to feel complete and aligned with mind, body, and spirit. When we spend time trying to fix and deny and hide entire dimensions of ourselves, we move out of that alignment.

This derails our best efforts and biggest dreams by leading us further from spirit. We do things like gossip and Facebook frequently. We drink too much and shop too much and work too much in an effort to avoid the uncomfortable feelings, the uncertainties, and the truth of all that we are.

These things work for a bit. They keep us busy so we have little time for introspection. But then those frivolous time wasters or addictions become one more reason to beat ourselves up, another imperfection that we have to go about fixing or hiding.

When we decide to see who we are, we become free. Then there is room for growth. We move from feeling trapped and stuck into a position of openness and gratitude for all that we are. We become more accountable for our actions and our lives.

Research by psychology professor Mark Leary indicates that people who admit their mistakes seem to rest easier, be more responsible, and more compassionate.

Understanding our imperfections frees us to explore different avenues of self-understanding and improvement. This is not mediocrity; it is movement. How far you go and how much you grow all depends on your motivation.

> # POWER UP:
> The contrast that comes from acknowledging your flaws and imperfections allows for greater compassion, accountability, and gratitude.

KNOWING YOUR MOTIVATION

Are you motivated to improve and change because you want to be self-actualized and authentic? Is it growth and expansion and well-being that you're after? Or are you making changes and doing things primarily because you want to sit high on the cultural totem of perfection? Is it the image you want or the insight?

There is no wrong answer here, but the practice of imperfection looks at self-improvement from the growth perspective.

If you want to fix your flaws because you want to be the hottie for your husband or impress the moms at the playgroup, or make more money, or fit in to some other external expectation, that's fine, but you have a whole lot of unfulfilling, hard work ahead of you.

To recognize whether you're motivated by insight or image, start asking yourself these questions:

When you look closely at your less-than-perfect parts, what do you see?

Can you laugh at or forgive some of your flaws? Can you embrace them?

What would you like to change or get better at? Why?

When you think of exploring that imperfect part of yourself, what do you feel? Curious, afraid, exhilarated? Relieved? Or exhausted?

If you answered exhausted for the last question, your motivation to change and grow and improve is probably more centered on fixing something for others instead of helping yourself develop. While the practice of imperfection is uncomfortable and scary at times, it is also invigorating. It won't wear you out. It will free you up.

When we embark on a process of self-discovery every experience becomes an opportunity for learning. Every challenge and hardship becomes a possibility for growth. It infuses our lives with vitality and meaning.

IN THE MOMENT PRACTICE:
CONNECTING TO YOUR SUCCESS

Take on this quick challenge while you're in the middle of a chore you'd rather not be doing. For me, unloading the dishwasher is a perfect time.

Think of a time when you achieved an important-to-you goal or marked a great success.

What was the achievement?

Now reflect on the challenges that surfaced while you worked toward your goal. What went wrong? What thwarted your progress? What did you overcome?

Perhaps there were technical mishaps or self-doubts. Maybe you came down with the flu or had a fight with your husband—whatever. Remember that the pursuit of this success wasn't always fun and easy peasy.

Now, reflect on the moment you completed it. What made that moment so profound? Why was it such an achievement?

Our biggest accomplishments are usually influenced by the mishaps and mistakes that occur along the way. It's part of the process. Recognize that the practice of imperfection is inherent to accomplishment.

BEGINNING THE PRACTICE

To take on the practices and strategies in this book, you've got to let loose a bit, drop your guard, and give up some of the rules that have kept you stuck.

Here are a few things that can help:

Drop the should-dos. We are surrounded by things we ought to do. Rules we should follow. Habits we must break. What if you did only what was important to you? For a while, do things because they feel right, not because someone says you should. Heck, if you want to wear white after Labor Day, put on the white pants. Of course, we'll all be talking about you, but who cares? This practice isn't about following some arbitrary rules to make others happy, no matter what your mom says.

Sit with the ick. Resist the urge to move out of the uncomfortable moments. From our caveman days (and no, I don't remember them), we learned to grab up our spears and go when something felt scary or cold or icky. Rarely, do we need to do that anymore. Instead, settle into the ick. Get curious about the discomfort and let it move through you. It may reveal some interesting truths.

Laugh. When I heard myself actually saying the words, "Don't put any more raisins up your nose," I felt like my life was being orchestrated by a group of writers bucking for sitcom laughs. But, when you think about it, those sitcom characters are endearing and well loved because of their flaws and their willingness to laugh at themselves. Try it. The dumbest things happen, but when we can laugh at ourselves, and the absurdities of our lives, everything gets easier.

Open up to the experience. Some of us—okay, me—are so busy micromanaging our lives that we forget to experience it. Go with the proverbial flow; pay attention to how you are feeling, what you're experiencing. Be open. This is when we can see the gold flecks sparkling out from all that ore.

As long as we are on the quest to be perfect, to fit some arbitrary image of the ideal person, we'll be stuck. Think hamster on a wheel, stuck. We'll be moving fast, sure. We'll be busy, busy, busy and we can even convince ourselves that we're super-important, but we won't be getting anywhere and we certainly won't be growing into our best selves.

The practice of imperfection is about living well with *all* of your qualities—your strengths and talents, your flaws and failings. It's about working with the success in your life and with the places where you don't have it all figured out. When we recognize the limits of perfection, we become more comfortable with our less than perfect behaviors. Living from this place of imperfection, then, becomes a power position, the path to wholeness.

PERENNIAL PRACTICE:
TAPPING INTO THE STRENGTH
OF IMPERFECTION

Pull out a journal—one that makes you feel good to write in—and spend at least twenty minutes playing with the ideas below.

Pick one thing you've always disliked or felt embarrassed about, a quality that you'd like to change.

Give it a color.

Now think of some of the times this color shows up in your life in beautiful ways. Write them down.

Then write down times this quality has also served as a strength. Be open to the possibility; look hard for it.

Perhaps you've always hated your passive demeanor and inability to share an opinion. You've painted it a wimpy pink, because it's made you feel weak. But pink is also the color of a stunning sunset and a delicate rose. And your passive demeanor may have been the very strength that helped you survive an abusive childhood. It protected you, made you sensitive to moods and tendencies of others. That information is invaluable when it comes to relationships.

Often, the very things we hope to rid ourselves of are essential to our development. Know that your flaws and failures have contributed to all the goodness that you are.

Give thanks for this quality, the one you've been frustrated by—it has served you.

ONE PATH:
LEARNING THROUGH MISTAKES

Growing up in rural West Virginia, things always seemed a little "off" to Richard Earls. His mother was unpredictable, often hysterical and angry. His father, though a local businessman, was frequently gone on out-of-town business trips and Richard grew up anxious and out-of-sorts. "It just wasn't a happy situation," he says.

When he was thirteen, Richard discovered one reason why: His mother and father were never actually married and his dad kept another family in another town twenty miles away. As far as his father's frequent business trips? "Those are the times he stayed with his other kids," Richard says, which created hostility between his parents.

When he was sixteen years old Richard left home. He hitchhiked to North Carolina where he enrolled in a boarding school, asking for permission and funding from his father only after he talked his way in.

He later married. "I was so young I think I was really emotionally retarded in some ways," he says, and then graduated from law school.

But that didn't feel right either. He hated practicing law and quit to begin a career as an entrepreneur, building and selling businesses.

By 2004, though, Richard appeared to be a success story. He'd been married for twenty-seven years, had money in the bank, lived in a fancy home, drove expensive cars, and lived the good life. That faded when Richard was fired from the company he had built and sold months before, lost his marriage, and went bankrupt. He found himself homeless, showering at the YMCA, and sleeping in the back of his Range Rover—one of the few things he still owned—until it was repossessed.

The change of fortune caused him to take a serious look at the messes and mistakes in his life: the family dysfunction, the failed business ventures, the broken relationships that seemed to plague him and his family.

"I asked, 'What is it that we [the Earls men] are doing that ends up making a wreck out of all the relationships and things around us?'" Richard says. "Not one of us had the capacity to hold onto anything for the long term and I wanted to figure that out and bring something better out of these mistakes. I had to take a hard look at myself to do that."

Introduced to a life coach by a woman he had begun dating, Richard began to shine a light onto everything in his life. Instead of blaming and complaining about the "bad luck" and "failures" in his life, he accepted full responsibility for all of it. Then he got proactive—went to therapy, attended seminars, began studying Jungian psychology—with the goal of becoming more self-aware.

"I realized that whatever was happening on the outside was reflected from the inside," Richard says. "I wanted to clean that up."

Richard says he emerged from the personal, spiritual, and financial bankruptcy more aware and conscious in his life. By waking up to all that was wrong, to all that was failing and falling apart, Richard found a way to something better.

As he began growing and learning about himself, he also began developing new businesses. Today, he runs two successful web-based marketing businesses catering to travel industry professionals and consumers. He's been in a fulfilling relationship for nearly eight years.

"The danger wasn't that I was going to quit on my life," Richard said. "The danger was that I would keep going on the way I was. I had to take a look at my mistakes and the ways that I was sabotaging myself and rebuild my life. I think I'm a better person than I was seven years ago, and I'm still growing."

"What a great teacher experience is," Richard says, "but man, it's also pretty brutal. I wish I'd started out a lot sooner, but I'm happy with where I am now. A lot of people die never really figuring out how to shape their life. I wanted to learn a better way."

Chapter 2:

Courage to Stand with Your Truth

We gain strength and courage and confidence by each experience in which we really stop to look fear in the face...we must do that which we think we cannot.

— ELEANOR ROOSEVELT

I saw George for nearly ten years. He was my go-to guy. We talked about life, shared stories, and then he raised his prices. I married and moved across town, and I knew it was time for a new stylist. The thought of telling George, though, of actually breaking up with him, made me sweat. I was afraid of how he would react. I didn't want to hurt his feelings.

I practiced what I would say in front of the mirror, and when I finally mustered the courage to say "goodbye," George was gracious and understanding. He gave me a parting hug and kiss. I turned and walked through the parking lot without looking back.

Breaking up with your hair stylist doesn't come close to running into a burning building or confronting a bully of a boss, but like so many of the little moments of our lives, it requires courage.

It can be tough to tell someone what they don't want to hear, to stand up for your beliefs, share your opinions, and keep going when you failed before. Whenever we risk failure, discomfort, or conflict, we draw from courage. It takes courage to cope with the changes of everyday life, to deal with the uncertainties, to do the right thing despite disapproval. It takes courage to live authentically. When you take a clear-eyed look at your life, courage can help you settle in with what you see.

THE CORE OF COURAGE

Daily life is filled with dozens of situations and experiences that draw from our reserves of courage: getting a mammogram, sharing difficult feelings, wearing your swimsuit, standing up to your kid's teacher, and saying "no" when everyone wants you to say "yes."

What's scary for me—breaking up with my stylist—may

seem ridiculous to you, but we all have different fears, percep-
tions, and vulnerabilities, so naturally we pull from our courage at different times. Courage, then, is a matter of perspective. But, "if you feel like something is a risk some courage is
probably required to cope," says Cynthia Pury, professor of
psychology at Clemson University, who studies the nature of
courage and how it shows up.

Researchers like Pury believe that courageous acts, whether minor or massive, usually require four things:

1. You must act voluntarily and on purpose.
2. The act usually takes place after some deliberation or
   thought (this doesn't have to take a lot of time).
3. You recognize some of the risks involved.
4. You are motivated by a "noble, good, or worthy end,"
   Pury says. That makes the action worth the risk.

In other words, if your stomach feels like jelly and you're afraid
that you'll go broke, flunk out, lose your job, or face a verbal
lashing, but you decide to start the business, have the baby, or
go back to school *anyhow,* you are acting courageously.

When you feel the fear *and* take the risk to push toward
that clear, meaningful objective, the experience alone illumi-
nates your essence and you are catapulted into a life that is full
of possibility.

Chances are you've already done this about a billion times, though you probably didn't define your actions as courageous. We usually reserve that word for firefighters and astronauts, though some courage is innate to each of us. Research also indicates that we can cultivate more.

The quality comes in handy when you take on the practice of imperfection because it gives you the guts to uncover all that you are and then use this ragout of mess and madness and creativity and love and curiosity and joy and uncertainty and insecurity to engage fully in your life. Courage makes it possible for you to share your feelings, pursue your passions, try new things, and love more than before.

This doesn't mean you won't feel afraid. I regularly feel that "I'm-not-enough" brand of panic when I try something new or face up to something meaningful. There is always a risk of feeling uncomfortable, embarrassed, unpopular, or lonely, but you don't choose a lesser life because of the fear. Instead, you muster the courage to move through the discomfort. Fear can't hurt you unless it stops you. Courage can help you keep going.

Of course, you can decide not to do any of this. You can settle safely into the status quo. Which is a nice way of saying you'll remain stuck. Instead of writing the screenplay that could be rejected, you'll critique sitcoms from your couch. Instead of applying for the promotion, you'll whine about how inept your boss is. Instead of going on that date, you'll complain that there are no good men left.

POWER UP:

There can be no forward motion without courage. Courage drives our willingness to work, engage, create, love, learn. Courage helps us tap into our own truth and live a more authentic life.

IN THE MOMENT PRACTICE: LIVING WITH COURAGE

Spend two minutes on this exercise to remind yourself that you've been brave before. It's in you.

Think of a time when you experienced a big change or transition. Perhaps you took a new job, got married, moved to a new city, went to graduate school, wrote a book, had a baby.

Remember how you felt during that time. Were you anxious? Excited? How did your body feel, tight or loose? Did you sleep well at night, or stay awake planning? Let yourself feel those emotions again.

Feel into any of the fear and anxiety you experienced

during that time. Even the things we're excited about often unleash some feelings of fear.

What did you do when you felt the fear?

What made you keep going?

Now move into a time just after the transition was completed. You made the move; you finished your first day on the job; whatever it was, remember the feelings that came with completion of your goal. Remember what it felt like to feel afraid and still get the job done.

See? You already have the courage and strength within you to launch your best life.

DIMENSIONS OF COURAGE

If you do decide to participate in this life, you'll not only realize the need for courage, but you'll see it showing up in all kinds of ways:

Physical Courage: This is the kind that requires you to put yourself in harm's way in the name of that good ol' noble goal. You might risk hypothermia or death by rescuing the dog from the ice flow, or charging into rough seas to rescue a doomed swimmer. For me, putting on roller skates to go to the rink with my daughter would require a super-sized meal of physical courage. Not kidding.

Moral Courage: When you stand up for what you believe though it might be unpopular with those around you, you are exhibiting moral courage. You risk disapproval, ostracism, and sometimes the loss of a friendship, job, or marriage, by doing what you believe is right. For example, confronting the boss over discrimination or taking a stand against your husband's drinking could result in unemployment or the end of a relationship.

Psychological Courage: If you find the strength to examine your life and transcend the challenges, transitions, and limiting behaviors, chances are you are pulling from my personal favorite in the courage category: psychological courage.

It doesn't require you to bound into a burning building, which is always a plus, I mean who really wants to do that, or stand up to the boss (though oftentimes all three types of courage interrelate), but it is needed when you decide to confront your own limiting beliefs, your insecurities, fears, anxieties, bad habits, and behaviors.

Psychological courage helps you acknowledge that:

Your two-drink-a-day diversion is now an alcohol *problem*.

You no longer love your husband.

You're staying in a job because you are afraid to make a change.

You are depressed.

I get that this is not the sexy side of courage. There is

something empowering and Ego-building about rescuing a child, and psychological courage doesn't feel all that heroic. It just feels hard to face up to the discomforts and imperfections that we've gotten so used to living with. But when you have the courage to look at yourself and all that baggage, you have a chance to discard what isn't working and align with spirit. You have a chance to live authentically. That's pretty heroic stuff.

TAPPING INTO YOUR PSYCHOLOGICAL COURAGE

Psychological courage gives us the strength to honestly see ourselves, and our circumstances. Instead of being afraid of the pain this truth may cause, we are courageous enough to experience it.

Doesn't mean we aren't scared. It's frightening to find the places where you are succumbing and numbing to bad behaviors and limiting beliefs. It's distressing to discover the ways you are sabotaging yourself, the areas of life where you are living a less-than existence. It's painful to realize you are not the person you think yourself to be.

But when you decide to stand up for your life and pull from your reserves of psychological courage to really see the failings and flaws and weaknesses and disappointments, you also get to see the joy and beauty and love and humor that is there too. We are all of that.

POWER UP:

Psychological courage allows you to confront a problem
or challenge or circumstance, despite profound discomfort, in order to solve it and create a better future.

Here's how it works: You want to feel healthier. But, before
you head to the gym, you decide to pull from your reserves of
psychological courage to explore why you are overweight to
begin with.

That's when you discover that you are an emotional eater.
You eat when you are feeling inadequate, which is often, because you have little self-worth. You explore this thought and
learn how your feelings were shaped by your past life experiences—the demanding father, the relationship that broke your
heart, your spouse's affair. You see clearly now why you're
overweight and you know that by looking at the truth of your
circumstance you can get a handle on it. It isn't comfortable to
have the demons and disappointments that you like to suppress
with food resurface. It isn't easy to acknowledge how you sold
yourself out. It is painful. But you are brave enough to look at
the reality and use it to shape a healthier experience.

It takes courage to move from avoidance or blame (I don't
have time to cook healthy meals) into awareness. But when you

make that shift, it almost always leads to inspired action.

Recognizing that you are an emotional eater with low self-worth may prompt you to seek counseling or other forms of support and self-knowledge.

Admitting that you aren't fulfilled in your successful, long-term career may inspire you to follow your heart into a dream job.

Acknowledging that your relationship is suffocating and stagnant can lead to a heart-to-heart with your partner, which might improve or change things.

When we courageously seek the truth, we step into our role as creators and innovators. We become inspiring as well as inspired. We become expansive, rather than constricted. We become pioneers discovering who we are and trusting who we will become.

There can be none of this growth without courage. And, as philosopher Dan Putman writes, "psychological courage is essential to happiness." Your job then is to uncover it, strengthen it, and use it to launch the rest of your life.

HOW COURAGE WORKS

When I was eight, I desperately wanted to jump from the side of the motel pool into the water. I still remember my fear. I fussed and danced around the water's edge, a ball of excitement and anxiety. It didn't matter that my tiny body was plugged into

a tight fitting inner tube or that my dad was in the water below ready to catch me or even that I could swim. I was totally
freaked about jumping. At the same time I knew I could do it.
I wanted to do it. I needed to do it, so that I could get off the
darn edge of the pool and start swimming.

> ## POWER UP:
>
> Each of us possesses some degree of courage and re-
> search indicates that you can actually build more. One
> way to do it is to continually take on tasks that feel a
> little scary or uncomfortable. Trust me, this gets easier
> with practice.

Life is like this. Sometimes we are blocked by the smallest, most
insidious things. We are stuck there standing on the edge worrying about what will happen if we jump, worrying about what
will happen if we don't, but never actually doing anything.

There is nothing wrong with being afraid. Fear is normal
and necessary and sometimes essential to our survival. But I'm
not talking about the kind of fear that keeps us safe from the
Boogie Man. I'm talking about the kind of fear that keeps us
stuck in a bad place, the fear that makes us less than we are
because we are afraid to look at what we could be.

The cloak of courage will never take away that fear but

you can recognize that, and by keeping your goal firmly in mind you can find the courage to face it down or live easier with it.

It took me awhile, but I did jump into the pool that day and my fear instantly turned to fun. I couldn't get enough. I kept jumping and jumping. That moment reminds me how foolish and real some of our fears can be. How they can keep us stuck inside ourselves. It reminds me too how much fun it can be to push beyond them. The more we do it, the braver, and more powerful we become.

IN THE MOMENT PRACTICE: GIVING CREDIT

Take a breath.

Think of a moment sometime in the last month or two when you took a small risk for a meaningful goal, one that ultimately had a successful outcome. Perhaps you took on a new work project, or had "The Relationship Talk" with someone you love, or signed up for a weight-loss program.

Now mentally list three emotions you felt before taking on the risky task.

Identify one thing you did to overcome it.

As you think back to that moment when you took that first step forward through the fear, what did it take for you to accomplish this goal?

What does it mean that you did it?

Feel all the positive feelings that came with doing something that felt so hard and scary to begin with.

Take a breath. Feel your power. Recognize you are courageous enough to take on anything.

SIX STEPS TO BUILDING COURAGE

The scariest things we encounter usually aren't sudden. We have a little time to prepare for the job interview. We can plan before we start our own business, or schedule the surgery, or set the wedding date. And during that lull between your decision to do something and the action you take, you can build the courage you need.

"People who say they acted courageously also talked about gearing up ahead of time," Pury says. They did something to boost their courage. You can too.

Here are some ways to do it:

1. **Remember the goal and recommit to it.** "People who hold their goal clearly in mind tend to be able to rise up and take courageous action despite feeling the fear," Pury says.

2. **Work to decrease your risk.** Plan, prepare, research, do whatever you need to do to prepare for the act you are undertaking. You'll never minimize all the risk, but you can eliminate some and that will make you feel better when fear sets in.

3. **Practice.** It's helpful to practice before pressing circumstances require it. Raise your hand in class, when

you would otherwise stay quiet. Say "no" to an invite, when you always say "yes." Run the race you're not sure you can finish.

By taking these baby steps in lower-risk situations you gain some courage and confidence and that helps you to cope when more difficult situations emerge.

4. **Give yourself some options.** Expect challenges to arise and get ready to deal with them. Fill in the blanks with an expected barrier and develop a plan: "If this happens, _____, then I will do this _____ to stay on track." Though you can't plan for every outcome, it's reassuring to know you have a few of them figured out.

5. **Acknowledge how you're feeling right now.** Feel the fear in the present, don't judge it or change it, or beat yourself up over it; just notice it and you'll see that you can survive it.

6. **After you take action, recognize that you did it.** Celebrate the effort, no matter the outcome. Remembering that you faced down your fear will help you do it the next time.

COURAGE IN THE MOMENTS

The grandest goals—raising a happy child, helping the less fortunate, building a business, living a healthy life, changing the world, and anything else we can imagine—are all made up of small moments. These little pieces of time and memory and emotion, like jumping off the edge of the pool, have a big impact on our lives. How we experience them determines the quality of the life we'll live.

You can turn away from these moments in the fear of uncertainty, change, and vulnerability. You can withdraw. Limit yourself. Play it safe. Or you can step into them—sometimes whining and fussing and crying and worrying—but moving forward just the same, and pulling on every ounce of courage you can muster to see the truth of your life. To be the whole of whom you are.

You've got this kind of courage in you. You've shown that simply by opening this book. By choosing to learn and grow and align with your spirit to step into your essence, even when it's scary.

I thought of how many times I needed courage in the moment on my daughter's first day of kindergarten. It took courage for me to let her climb onto that massive piece of steel and motor and fuel and energy that we call a bus. Sweet P was feeling it too—the fear and excitement that often comes up in the changing moments of our lives, just before we call on our courage.

"My tummy feels a little funny," she said. "I think I'm feeling a little scared."

I felt her fingers wrap around mine as we plodded to the bus stop. "It's because I don't know what it's like, Mama. But that's okay because I'll just do it and then I can figure it out."

If you're willing to do the same, take on whatever makes your tummy feel funny, if you are willing to draw from your courage to explore your disappointments and setbacks, to shed your public image to discover your authentic self, and move in the direction of your heart and spirit, you'll gain access to the peace and power that comes with acceptance, and connect to the energy of everyday life.

PERENNIAL PRACTICE:
PRACTICING COURAGE

Pull out a pen and journal and spend about twenty minutes for this exercise. It's a nice one to do first thing in the morning so that you can use the awareness to guide your day.

Sit down and list three things that are working well in your life. You'll know what they are because just thinking about them prompts good feelings.

Now identify one thing that isn't so hot. Just one.

Need a little more kindness or romance in your relationship? Is your body out of shape? Bored at work?

Pinpoint something that is lacking and write that down.

Now take a deep breath. Sit quietly and think about that area of lack.

Get specific about what isn't working right. Get clear about the letdown, the excuses, and the blame that may be limiting you in this area.

How have you contributed to that area of lack? How are you responsible for the failure or imperfection? How have you let yourself down?

Be gentle, but recognize your role in the failure.

Write down one thing you must do, or one of the habits or behaviors that you must change to bolster this area of lack.

What feels scariest about doing so? What is the risk of changing this thing?

Now write down one thing you could do to prepare for this risk.

Remind yourself of why you want to make this change. Think about what your life will feel like when you do it. Keep your goal in mind.

Then do it. Have the talk with your husband. Sign up for a gym membership. Go on that date.

Celebrate yourself and the courage you showed to acknowledge the lack in your life and take inspired action to change it.

ONE PATH:
COURAGE TO SPEAK

Ann Quasman knew it was a knife long before she felt its blade slash her skin.

She'd finished shopping and was ready to load the groceries into her car around 9:30 p.m., on an evening nearly thirty years ago. She felt its tip in her back just before she was forced into her car and ordered to drive to a remote location where for two-and-a-half hours she was raped and cut with the knife.

Finally, Ann says, the man took a break and got out of the car. That's when she found the courage to make her escape. Until that moment, she'd been virtually paralyzed and silent during the ordeal. But now she fumbled for the keys that he'd tossed on the floorboard, locked the doors, and with shaking hands, started the car. It was her only chance to get away. Later the assailant was arrested and sentenced to prison.

Ann's physical wounds healed, but she rarely talked about the experience. In those days she rarely spoke out about anything and certainly didn't talk publicly about the attack.

Even as a child, she dreaded public speaking. The thought left her nauseous with hives. She took classes to try to overcome her fear, and later, as a finance executive and senior vice president of a major financial institution, she took Valium to numb the anxiety, right along with the prescription pain medications she used for two decades to deal with chronic pain from a car accident years earlier. Between twelve-hour-plus workdays and the drugs, Ann says she lost sight of herself.

"I finally just realized I had no idea what was going on in my body," says Ann, who is now fifty-nine. "I was not eating or sleeping right, I weighed less than a hundred pounds. Things just weren't right. I was disconnected and numb."

It was a scary time, but with encouragement and intervention from a friend, Ann began working to reclaim her health. She stopped taking the prescription drugs, and when the pain came raging back, she used acupuncture and physical therapy to cope.

She got married, left her job, and permanently slowed down her life. She began to uncover her spiritual side. She learned yoga, took up journaling, and began practicing meditation. The greatest relief from her pain came from the Emotional Freedom Technique (EFT).

After a year of tapping to open up the body's energy points, Ann's pain was gone and so was her former life. Ann continued her intense personal and spiritual studies, which led her to teach self-healing classes to small groups of women.

When she realized that so many others had endured sexual assault, Ann began to tell her story. She found her voice and used it to help others.

Those classes have evolved into a weekly radio show,

Woman Talk Live, in Baltimore, where the Lutherville, Maryland, woman who, for years, kept her silence, is the voice of reason and wisdom and empowerment for women across the country.

"I was afraid to do it; I was petrified," Ann says, "but I did it and you know it's been my passion since day one."

Today, as well as hosting the show, Ann also serves on the board of the Maryland Coalition Against Sexual Assault (MCASA) and appears and speaks at scores of public events.

"I think there must really be a reason why I'm still here," Ann says. "There were plenty of times that I was scared, really scared, but fear is not going to ruin my life or run my life. I just feel like I have some bone of resilience. I am just not going to give up. And, you know now, I'm right where I need to be."

Chapter 3:

Working with What Is

The Master takes action in letting things run their
courses.

—*Tao Te Ching*,
TRANSLATED BY STEPHEN MITCHELL

MY PATH TO ACCEPTANCE

Sweet P started crowing on the baby monitor around 6
a.m., long before I was ready to open my eyes. I listened to
her awhile, trying to stretch and loosen my aching joints
enough to climb out of bed without falling.

I am Tin-Man stiff in the mornings. When I was three, I

was diagnosed with Juvenile Rheumatoid Arthritis. Over the years it has invaded nearly every joint between my neck and toes. It took years before I could see the knuckles in my hands, and longer still before I could function without heavy medication. Today my mornings are just plain messed up. My body is slow and achy and stiff. Walking is tough. But I've learned to get by. I've learned to thrive.

I did well in school, in spite of the arthritis. I played basketball, in spite of the arthritis. I traveled, worked my dream job, got married, had a child, and golfed, all in spite of the arthritis. These days I live a grand and productive life, with few complaints, in spite of the arthritis. The disease taught me more than it took from me. And I went through life, refusing to give it much attention.

I rarely even talked about it, seldom asked for help. To do so, to mention the pain and grief, was to give the disease power, I believed.

Many days, I denied how difficult it was. This worked just fine, until that chilly morning in the spring of 2007 when Sweet P crowed from her crib.

I pushed myself out of bed, leaning against the wall for support until I reached her bedroom where I lurched from the doorknob to the dresser to the knob on the corner of her crib, barely able to get my ankles to bend enough to keep my balance. But, this time when I saw her something changed. In that moment, I understood that to continue denying my disease was flat-out dangerous.

All these years I had willed my body to do what it struggled to do. I had invested everything into my mind and spirit hoping to compensate for and blot out the pain of my physical imperfection. But on that morning, I knew that if I leaned over to pick up this precious baby in spite of the arthritis, even while I was weak and unsteady, I was jeopardizing the one person who needed me to be better, more truthful than that.

I wasn't willing to do it. I wasn't willing to risk falling or dropping her to prove I could fight through the illness. It was time to get real.

I reached over her crib rail and rubbed her head. We played with the musical lamb and I stretched and limbered up. I sat down in the rocking chair, and my husband came in and lifted her into my arms. She squirmed and pushed off my shoulder looking at the world around her, and I grieved for the moments that I couldn't do it all, and for a body that would never be easy. I grieved the loss of my health, though it had been altered years before. And, in that moment, I gave thanks for all that I did have, all that I was. On that morning, I accepted it all.

> ## POWER UP:
>
> With resistance comes stress, pain, limitation. Acceptance offers clarity, awareness, peace. From that place decisions are easier.

Acceptance had eluded me all these years and I didn't even know it. Until I was able to acknowledge the disease and all that it had done to and for my body, I was stuck living in spite of. I was living in a place of resistance, with some fear of being found out. Afraid of not being enough—that's a stressful way to go. To accept the arthritis meant relief, clarity. It meant I could operate from a place of power and align with my spirit.

Acceptance is peace. Resistance is pain.

RESISTANCE HURTS

Look at the times you've been mad or hurt. Were they a result of missed expectations, ideas that didn't pan out, dreams you held in a death grip? Did you have a clear vision of how you wanted things to go and then, blip, they fell apart and so did you? Instead of accepting what actually did occur, you lamented what should have been. That's resistance.

"If things are ucky and icky, there's probably some resistance there," says psychotherapist, author, and former Buddhist monk Donald Altman. "You can fight it and suffer or you can take an attitude of acceptance and see what is and live from that place."

Consider the moments when things feel hard. Nothing flows. Projects fall through, you forget appointments, have computer problems. You have a flat tire, your cat throws up, and you lose your keys. Or the days when nobody seems to understand what you are trying to say, you feel drained, disconnected. Yet you soldier on. Push forward with the plan. Fight through challenges. Battle back from adversity (note even the language we use when we resist—battle, push, fight—sounds adversarial, rather than effortless) all the while wishing things were easier. All the while denying the reality of your circumstances. Denying that you need to change course, try something different, take a break, give up. When you're fighting against reality or wishing it away, that's resistance at work.

STAYING STUCK IN RESISTANCE

Resist anything long enough and the problems become bigger than forgotten appointments and flat tires. Resistance shows up as cracks in your marriage, headaches at work, cold viruses, stress, anger, alcoholism, cancer, and so much more. You drop antibiotics and aspirin and you push on coping, enduring, trying, blaming, lamenting, regretting, but never really moving through the hard stuff.

Sound familiar? We do this so well, this resistance thing, that we often don't realize we're being buried by it. Resistance is a speed bump in the middle of your spiritual path. It's like trying to cram into a size 8 when you've long been wearing a size 10. You can keep at it, after all, some styles run big, but the truth of it is, the pants don't fit. And, girl, they aren't gonna fit until you accept that you are no longer a size 8 and you buy a different size or get that body to the gym.

It isn't always bad. Resistance can keep you from eating your child's entire bag of Halloween candy while he sleeps, because you don't want to disappoint the kid (or admit that you really did eat the whole thing). Resistance can keep you from dating the bad boy, strapping on a bungee cord and plunging off a cliff, or having another child (which may feel like roughly the same thing).

But let's get real. Most of our resistance, denial, and avoidance comes from our fear of change and our attachment to desire. If you keep this up, a couple of things will happen: 1. You will stay stuck in the misery and limitation that you know, and 2. You'll probably get sick—your body will just plumb wear out due to the pressure and stress of living in resistance.

In one study, Gregory Miller, PhD, a researcher from the University of British Columbia, found that people who gave up on an insurmountable goal or obstacle felt better than those who pushed harder to reach the goal even when it was clearly unachievable. Those who kept fighting the reality and didn't accept defeat experienced greater inflammation and their bodies pulsed with higher levels of the stress hormone cortisol. Over time, that cortisol causes big problems, including a risk for heart disease, diabetes, and other chronic illnesses.

It's time to give up the fight in your life. Take a clear look at your circumstances, accept what you find, and be free to work with all that is to create a for-real life.

PATTERNS OF RESISTANCE

Take a minute now to look at the things in your life that aren't going according to your plan. You want to lose the weight, but can't seem to overlook the candy bar at the checkout stand. You wish you had a little more romance in your relationship, but don't know how to bring it up, so you say nothing and cozy up to a book instead of your partner.

Resistance, in a very real way, shows up as blocks in your life. It appears in the form of the same old problems, ongoing arguments, issues that never seem to resolve but always seem to matter—the twenty pounds you are unable to lose, the resolutions you repeat annually, the excuses you make. Because our pockets of resistance become familiar behavior and a habitual way of living, we often fail to notice that we're resisting at all.

Once you do tune in and gently look for the places resistance may be rooted in your life, you'll see some distinctive patterns. Resistance is almost always focused around our fears.

We will do just about anything to stay out of emotional and physical pain, which is often ignited by change, uncertainty, and social isolation. We don't want to hurt, we don't want to fail or be rejected, we don't want to feel embarrassed, lonely, or left out. So, we resist, deny, and avoid anything that forces us to face those fears. Ultimately, that traps us in the very things we're trying to avoid.

Perhaps you're feeling overwhelmed by work and kids and paying the bills and meeting the other demands of daily life. You get frequent colds, and always feel tired. You complain. Yet, every time a friend offers support or solutions you rattle off a bunch of excuses about how there's not enough money, not enough time, no way to change. Could those excuses and disclaimers be masquerading as resistance to fear and uncertainty? Maybe you're resisting the notion of change. Perhaps you feel more comfortable living with the chaos that you know, rather than adjusting your priorities and evaluating the personal imperfections that allow it to continue. Maybe you are afraid to ask for help. Or you believe you are incapable of doing something different or unworthy of something better. Maybe, too, you're not willing to do the work to change. That's okay. It's all okay, as long as you're honest and accepting. But, instead of being honest and clear about our circumstances, we resist and deny them. We make excuses and get caught up in the stories we create, stories that are always pure fiction.

When you see what is, when you have the courage to look at the reality rather than resisting it, you can begin to uncover the patterns that are keeping you locked down. Then they start to break up and dissolve. There is relief in this. You find out that the things you fear aren't all that scary. You begin to live consciously, with the awareness of what is, rather than judgment. And pain is transformed to peace.

ACCEPTANCE IS THE ANTIDOTE

Famed psychologist Carl Jung summed it up like this, "What you resist, persists. But acceptance is freedom."

Here's how it works: If my husband doesn't clean the food scraps out of the sink after he does dishes, I don't like it. I resist the notion of a dirty, grimy sink. That resistance shows up through various unhelpful statements, like "I can't believe you NE-VER clean the sink," followed up by plenty of feelings of annoyance and frustration—which are then expressed during a lecture—complete with a sink-wiping demonstration. While all of this makes me look totally ridiculous (yes, I get that), none of it actually gets the sink clean. I know. I've tried it—repeatedly.

Or I could always go with Plan B and just accept that the sink is gunky. A dirty sink doesn't have to be anything bigger than that. It's not an indication of my husband's love, or a sign that the next global health epidemic will begin in our kitchen. Dirty sinks are, in fact, just dirty sinks. When I get this and accept it, something crazy happens—I wipe out the damn sink.

My husband sees me doing it, apologizes for forgetting the chore, and we talk about how a clean sink, in some odd way, makes me feel more at ease. I stop nagging. He becomes a sink cleaner.

Not everything has to have a story. Not everything has to be bigger than it is. Life is pretty clear when we don't inflate it with rhetoric and drama and resistance.

IN THE MOMENT PRACTICE:
FEELING THE RESISTANCE

Stop where you are and take five minutes for this experiment. No supplies needed.

Be still. Pay attention to what is feeling good in your life in this moment. Make a mental note of the areas where things feel easy and in flow. Note, too, where your experience is just the opposite, where things feel tight, hard.

Physical tightness indicates emotional resistance. What are you stressed about, defensive about?

Are you resisting reality?

Can you let it go? Can you see the truth and all that it is and let it be?

Wouldn't that feel better?

Try it.

When you don't accept things as they are, you are pushing up against the Universe, trying to unravel what's done, wishing away what already is. This is exhausting and it makes no sense. To make choices from this place is akin to buying a pair of jeans you've never seen; who would do that?

Yet, we buy in to all kinds of things—relationships, careers, bodies—without honestly looking at the reality before us. We create stories: "My job isn't that bad," "He doesn't mean to treat me that way," "I'm just big-boned" to keep us rooted to our resistance.

How can you move closer to spirit, without knowing where you are to begin with? Acceptance offers this kind of clarity.

GETTING CLEAR

Acceptance takes you out of that pattern of pain and resistance. It is not giving in. It is not giving up. Acceptance is not resignation. "It's getting clear about what the reality is, to allow the moment to be without any resistance whatsoever," says Martha Beck. She describes it as, "saying yes to the mess."

Accepting the situation doesn't mean you need to put up with bad behavior or dangerous conditions. It means only that you see the situation for what it is. When you do this you get out from under the disappointment of missed expectations and new possibilities become visible.

Sometimes, it's the difference between life and death. It is always the difference between an authentic life and one leashed by delusion.

If you're tossed in the middle of the lake, for example, you can only tread water for a few minutes before you become a little desperate. You can spend that few minutes saying things like,

"This is all *his* fault." Or, "It isn't fair." Or, "Wearing a swimsuit always gets me into trouble," and you'll still be out there in the middle, tired of treading water. Or you could accept that you're in trouble and call for help, or start swimming for shore.

You don't need to wail about your hatred for water or even claim to be happy about swimming. Acceptance is not a judgment call. It doesn't require an opinion or even any special skills. You need only to honestly evaluate the situation, and let go of the story you've created around it. Then you are free to make a move and you'll be clearer about which direction to take.

POWER UP:

Acceptance allows for forward motion. When you clearly see your circumstances, you have accurate information to use to move beyond them.

NO JUDGMENT REQUIRED

Acceptance does require you to let go of judgment. This is a toughie because we have become universally good at analyzing, commenting, predicting, judging everyone from the driver who cuts us off on the freeway to the kid who sings in his shower on YouTube. Sometimes we forget we don't have to do it at all. We don't have to judge or criticize. In fact, here's a shocker—most often nobody's asking our opinion.

Yet when we judge something, resistance takes root. We are hardwired to resist pain so we try to escape anything we judge as painful or bad or scary. We tap into subversive getaway strategies, like criticism, avoidance, defensiveness, anger, blame, and procrastination, to disconnect from what is in the present and move further away from peace and acceptance.

To accept something means to accurately identify the situation. Speak the bare-bones truth without opinion. The counter is not clean—that's the reality. The thought, "My husband is a jerk who doesn't love me enough to clean the counters," is a massive faulty judgment that leaves me feeling bad and certainly doesn't get the counters any cleaner.

I have rheumatoid arthritis. That's all it is. "I'm weak and sick and a terrible mother who can't do anything," is the lie that limits my potential.

THE LIES WE TELL

We lie to ourselves all the time. It's our way of denying and resisting, and sometimes protecting ourselves. But it's not an effective way. These lies are simply a part of the illusion we create to buffer us against our fears or insecurities. We use them to mask our imperfections so that perhaps we won't be discovered for who we really are—a flawed human being. But get this: who you are when you stand in your truth is always more powerful than the lies you create to hide it. Those lies always stunt our growth and keep us from living authentically.

Sometimes they are so subtle and so wholly believable that we fail to notice we're concocting a fictional story around our behavior. We say, "I'd love to write a book, but I just don't have the time," though we know we would make the time if we weren't afraid of the rejection. Other times our lies are in-your-face obvious, "I'm just not good enough," or "I can't lose weight, I'm big boned." Left unchecked, lies like these seep into our thought patterns and become part of our belief systems.

When we can shake off these lies and get real with ourselves, it becomes easier to live from a place of personal truth and integrity. This allows for movement and openness because we can channel all the energy we've used to lie and resist to now create a real experience, one that we truly want to live.

Instead of saying you want to lose weight, maybe it's time to acknowledge that you don't really care all that much and that you aren't willing to cut out the chocolate just now. That's okay. You don't have to judge that feeling or deny it; simply replace the lie, "I want to lose fifteen pounds," with the truth, "I weigh one hundred and fifty pounds," and accept it as is.

Rather than repeating that you don't have time to write the book, take the class, apply for the job, climb the mountain, do whatever it is, you could acknowledge that you are afraid, or not ready to make the commitment it requires to reach such a lofty goal. It's all good.

When you hold yourself accountable and accept what is, then you can also recognize that you are the creator of your own life and you can decide to reshape it at any time. You have a choice. You can continue the lies. Stay stuck in the illusion. Or you can accept reality, and free yourself up to experience it.

THE PRACTICE OF ACCEPTANCE

Start by paying attention. What's going on? Are you snappy and impatient? Do you sleep well or poorly at night? Hungry all the time or is your stomach upset? Finding it hard to focus? If you see a pattern of dead ends, uncomfortable feelings, or over-the-top responses, chances are resistance is at work in your life.

Uncover the truth. When you've identified the pockets of resistance in your life, you can see what's behind them. If you're overweight, the Ding Dongs in the cupboard are only part of the problem—what is causing you to eat them? Loneliness, insecurity, despair? Don't beat yourself up over your truth. There is no judgment to be cast. Just see what the reality is.

With this awareness, you have a choice. You can continue the route of resistance, or you can accept the reality and settle into it differently.

Declare your truth. Write it down. Say it out loud. Be clear about what's going on in your experience. Start simply, for example:

The sun is out today.

I ate a turkey sandwich for lunch.

I drive a Honda.

(**Then go deeper, get real.**)

I weigh more than I want.

I need help.

I'm unhappy in my marriage.

I'm not that good at my job.

I drink three glasses of wine a night.

My husband hits me when he's angry.

I don't want to work anymore.

I'm depressed.

Now you know. Read over your list. You can see the truth, right there before you. Remember, it's not a good or bad thing. You don't have to judge or associate any emotion to your reality. This is simply a declaration of what's happening now. And once you see it, you have the information you need to do it differently—or not.

Acceptance leaves room for action. It gives you a chance to fix what you can, make changes, or decide not to do anything at all. It also is a base camp for peace. You no longer have to fight or push, or excuse, or hide, or control. You don't have to put up with it either. You can accept that your father is an alcoholic without judgment or anger. When you stop resisting his behavior by denying or fighting it, you are free to choose what to do next. You can decide not to be around him when he is drinking, you can get the help you need to learn how to live with his alcoholism, you can encourage him to get treatment, or you can decide to do nothing at all.

When I moved into full acceptance of my arthritis, I made some immediate changes. I became more open and honest with my husband when I needed help. I began talking more truthfully about my experience—even on the bad days. I began a kinder, gentler approach to exercise. I began to work with the arthritis, instead of in spite of it, and I became much more self-compassionate.

ACCEPTANCE WHEN YOU'RE READY

Acceptance is a choice you can make at any moment. It's a conscious action that you take when you're ready. Sometimes it takes us awhile, because we have different layers to sort through before we're able to see. Some of us even have to overcome our resistance to the idea that we're resisting anything at all. I felt so familiar with the arthritis that it was almost unbelievable that I would deny any part of it. But, with practice, acceptance can happen in a moment. Open up to it, and enjoy the peace that comes.

IN THE MOMENT PRACTICE:
SAY WHAT YOU SEE

Use this five-minute exercise to begin your practice of acceptance. Have fun. This life-changing spirituality stuff doesn't have to be so serious.

Look around the room right now and say what you see, without judgment. Just see what's there: Dirty dishes in my sink. Food Network on the television. A big honking cobweb hanging from the skylight. Just list off the truth before you and do it without judgment.

When you get in the habit of seeing what's there, step your practice up a notch and use it in other areas of your life. Instead of "that checker was rude," the reality may be, "that checker did not talk to me." Acceptance simply says it like it is and leaves the rest behind.

"You don't have to create a story around life," says psychotherapist and author Donald Altman. You can just live it.

RELEASE AND SURRENDER

Once you are clear about what really is in your life you can decide to hold onto it or let it go. Buddha says, "Attachment is the source of all suffering." Anytime we hold tight to an idea, or thing, or person, or something we love and covet, we are resisting the reality, because everything is impermanent. The things we love will change or vanish altogether. We suffer, too, when we cling to our challenges rather than accepting and moving through them. Surrender, then, is the way to go. That doesn't mean it's always easy, but it is a path that becomes smoother with knowledge.

"Surrender is a voluntary thing," Altman says. It is a choice to let go in some way: to give up your worries and your troubles; to realize you don't have control. It is not submission. It is active—you are making a choice for release.

In other words, surrender means you have to stop multi-tasking and micromanaging. You have to loosen your grip a bit and believe that the Universe will be okay if you can't make it to every meeting. Peace comes when we give up this control. When we surrender to what is.

PERENNIAL PRACTICE: LETTING GO

Take fifteen minutes to get in the flow of accepting and letting go. By practicing on the little things, we become better at doing it during the troubling times.

Write down one thing that's driving you crazy—your husband's underwear on the floor, the scratch on your kitchen counter, the fact that you didn't get a workout in today or yesterday or anytime in the last year.

Take a breath, now, just accept it as it is.

Take a deep breath; exhale. Relax your body. Feel the air releasing. Do it again.

Say to yourself or out loud: "I'm releasing the _____ (scratch or whatever your little annoyance is). I'm giving it over to the Universe."

Now imagine breathing in that irritant—the scratch on the counter—then exhale and push it out. Let it dissipate in the air.

Feel the air and the irritant rushing out of your body. It's gone.

Sit in the quiet.

Write down how you feel.

With acceptance and surrender, we don't have to hold on to the hurt. We see what's going on, we allow it to be without judgment, and we release what isn't working.

HOW TO SURRENDER

To give up our attachments and disconnect from our desires (I'm not saying desires are bad, in fact, I'm all for them; it's our attachment to them that keeps us stuck and frustrated) to let go of our stories, and our pain, and our projections of what we think our life ought to be, is a relief.

> **POWER UP:**
>
> Surrender is a choice. It's a decision you make to release the interior garbage without expecting anything in return. You just let it go so you're not bogged down by it anymore.

These troubles you've been carrying around, no longer have to be your troubles. You can release them. In the beginning, after you decide to do this, your mind will kick in with its Emergency Alert System. This is your Ego fighting for its life, urging you to hold tight, keep working, try harder, and stay in control. It's worried that if you surrender, you will lose sight of who you are, your ideas, and drive, and desire. If you release your anxiety and worry, your Ego will say, it means you don't care enough. This is hogwash. Surrender actually makes room for more positive action. It leaves you free from the weights of worry so you can do something proactive.

Wouldn't it be nice, for example, to let go of your judgment about your weight? You can weigh two hundred pounds without beating yourself up. Instead of judgment, you can accept your weight *and* release the pain, disappointment, and attachment around it. Without the pain and stress, you are more likely to treat yourself with compassion. People with self-compassion make healthier decisions. Surrendering to the weight can actually help you release it in a very physical way.

Surrender is when we stop trying so hard. It frees us up to make a move without getting clobbered by the same pain over and over again.

When you let go of control, you are in effect handing it off to a higher energy, nature, God, the Universe, Source, whatever it is for you. You are letting go so that you can become centered in a place of health and well-being.

THE BODY'S PLACE IN SURRENDER

Often we become so attached to our conditions that it can be hard to find that place of surrender until we change our physiology and environment.

Move your body to a place or environment that represents peace and quiet and safety.

This can be a special spot in your house or a beautiful outdoor location. It helps me to sit along the ocean's edge or to look out at the stars. Nature is an obvious reminder that the Universe can handle whatever we cast off just fine. Then ask, quietly to yourself, or out loud at the top of your lungs, for what you want. Ask for healing, or support during the uncertainty, or a release from the pain and struggle. Get clear on what it is you are letting go.

Set the intention to release it: "I am releasing all this pain and my attachment."

Finally, let it go.

THE SOUL'S PURPOSE IN SURRENDER

This is where you allow your essential self to emerge. You align with your spirit as you release all the stuff you've been carrying around. You let go with the knowing that there is a bigger force here to guide you and help you. You are reminded that you are a spiritual being and you are finally able to see the blessings that are apparent within the pain.

But, here's the clincher, "you must release without expectation," Altman says. You can pray on what you need, contemplate the surrender, set the intention, get clear, but then, you must finally let go without expecting anything in return.

There are countless stories of people who have experienced miraculous healings, deep-seated peace, and tremendous relief in this process of surrender. There are also plenty of stories from people who felt nothing at all. Be open to whatever appears and remember that no matter how easy or hard it feels, surrender causes a psychic and spiritual shift. That's enough to make a difference in your life.

THE MIND'S PURPOSE IN SURRENDER

After you've turned your troubles over to the Universe, you may feel some balance restored, some peace and optimism. Right until you walk into the house and see the cat throw up on the couch or the bill on the counter. You'll feel all spiritual and connected to the Universe right until real life enters in again. This is where your mind—with some careful direction from your spirit—can help. Do not let it run away with you. Use your thoughts here to guide you in support of your surrender, to remind you (over and over again if needed) of what you released and the freedom that exists in that.

In the end, after all the angst and struggle over control, our move from resistance to acceptance, to surrender, actually shows us the blessings in the very moments we were once wishing away. We can see then, that all of this stuff—the messy and the marvelous, the pristine and imperfect—are part of our spiritual path and we can choose beliefs that support our spiritual growth.

ONE PATH:
FROM PAIN TO PEACE

Kelly James-Enger, forty-five, desperately wanted to be a mother and she always imagined having two children. After six years of infertility and four miscarriages, she and her husband decided to adopt. Their son arrived in 2005 and life was sweet and full.

"I just felt so grateful," Kelly said. "And I was so happy to be a mom. But there was still this part of me that wanted another child." So, eighteen months later, the couple decided to pursue a second adoption. This time it proved an arduous and painful path.

Over three years the family sent out thirty letters to pregnant women who were considering adoption, they were matched with expecting women four times, and once held a newborn who they expected to adopt minutes before the birth mother changed her mind. It was a time of broken promises and broken hearts.

"I was heartbroken and angry that we'd gone through so much and it wasn't happening. But I realized I needed to accept that I was the mother of an only child and probably always would be," Kelly says.

"I struggled at first. I went to therapy and worked out my feelings. I talked with my husband, my mom, and my closest friends. And I prayed a lot. I prayed not for another baby, but for peace. Finally, I was able to accept—and even get excited about—the idea of raising an only child. I could even see that there were benefits to having one child that I hadn't considered before."

For Kelly, acceptance and surrender was an active process. She lived with it consciously for months, exploring her feelings, sitting with the emotions, releasing the need for the ideal outcome. She prayed and turned her attachment over to her god.

"I remember saying that 'If you put a baby in my arms, I will say yes,'" Kelly says. "But, I wasn't actively looking for a child anymore. I was moving on, and was focused on the goodness that was already in my life." She prepared to close her adoption license, officially ending the search for another child.

That's when the call came. A friend knew a young woman who was considering adoption for her baby. It was a complicated situation, far from Kelly's home in Illinois, and it came just when she'd finally accepted her circumstances and made peace with her life as it was. This time, though the process did include moments of stress and anxiety, Kelly found peace, by surrendering to the situation.

"If this baby joined our family, I knew it would be wonderful," Kelly said. "But I also knew that even if that didn't happen I would be okay, that my family would be okay. I gave up the fight of it all."

Three months later, Haley was born and Kelly and her husband were there to hold their five-hour-old daughter.

Kelly doesn't believe that her acceptance led to the

adoption. But it did make her reality easier to live with during the process.

"It did take time to reach a place of acceptance. But when I finally did, I was able to embrace feelings of peace and gratitude and let go of the anger and sadness I'd had for so long. It was one of the hardest things I've ever done, but that is what finally gave me peace."

Chapter 4:

Building Powerful Beliefs and Cutting Catastrophic Thoughts

For those who believe, no proof is necessary.
For those who don't believe, no proof is possible.

—STUART CHASE

What is your back-up plan?" asked my boss, when I told him I was quitting the well-paying, soul-sucking public relations job to write full-time.

"I don't really have a back-up plan," I said. "I'm willing to deliver papers or something."

He looked at me, jammed his hands into his pockets, grinned, and slowly shook his head.

"I guess you're in trouble then, because you are never going to make it."

Okay, so he *was* a little bitter, but he wasn't totally off base. Starting any new business is not without risk and there are plenty of writers who don't make a living at it. But I had a secret weapon: I believed I could do it. Fortunately, that was enough.

Our beliefs underlie and influence everything we do and everything we are. Doubt their impact? Try to get a Democrat to vote for a Republican and you're likely to run up against a slate of powerful beliefs. The power of our beliefs has nothing to do with whether they are true—most aren't. It's how tightly we cling to them that allows them to shift our energy and shape our lives.

HOW BELIEFS WORK

We are belief magnets. Every action we take is based on our belief system. Our emotions evolve out of them, our relationships, our self-image, it's part of how our ancestors survived those early days on the savanna secure in their natural fiber cave fashions. When someone in the clan would become sick or die after eating a red berry, the others would quickly establish the belief that red berries are very, very bad. When a hunter in the group toppled over the edge of a cliff, caveman minds would click: "Ah, don't do heights."

Evolution isn't the only process shaping our beliefs without us knowing. Parents, teachers, friends, television shows, backs of cereal boxes, shoe salesmen and everything else—including our own choices and experience—influence how we think about things. Yet rarely do we examine those thoughts. Instead, we quickly interpret all the incoming information, assign it an emotion, respond with an action, and then begin repeating those same thoughts over and over.

Beliefs are simply those thoughts repeated so frequently that they become bionic, super-charged ideas affecting how we respond to everything in our lives. Our lives become tethered tightly to both the conscious and unconscious beliefs we hold, and often, we don't even realize it's happening.

Here's how it works:

You believe you're more fun when you drink, so you drink a lot in social situations.

You believe that it's important to help others, so you volunteer at the local food bank.

You believe you are unlovable, so you stay with a man who beats you.

You believe that your Dad was right when he said you were a fatty, so you routinely fill up on junk food and live out that belief.

You believe that you are a product of the Divine Source, loving and kind and worthy of abundance in all areas of your life. So, guess what? You have a family that loves you, a job that fulfills you, physical health, and money in the bank.

Like all the other beliefs you hold, this last one can become your reality.

Your beliefs become tangible, when you begin acting on those thoughts. Since they are the foundation of all that we do, it's not handy when you hold a belief that is limiting, irrational, unrealistic, or just plain wrong. When they fall into these categories, they become limiting beliefs that can cause big problems.

POWER UP:

Though many of our core beliefs are imprinted on us at an early age, you can change those by replacing the limiting ones with a new shinier set that energizes and inspires you.

This is like building a sandcastle on the high-tide line. You know that it's just a matter of time until that castle is swept out to sea. You wait for that wave, always looking over your shoulder. And you don't go to any extra trouble to create something magnificent. There is no tower or cupola on this castle. You limit yourself. It's all going to be washed away by the next wave, so what's the point—right? Bad stuff always happens to you. You've got the worst luck.

Psychologist Albert Ellis based his therapeutic approach, Rational Emotive Behavior Therapy, on this notion that irrational beliefs are at the root of our problems. And it's easy to see how that plays out in our everyday lives.

The good news about these rotten beliefs is that they are not true. They are illusions made real only by the actions we take. By choosing different beliefs, your actions change and so does your life.

"Don't allow abstract ideas and fake beliefs to overwhelm reality," says Martha Beck. "Anything that keeps you from feeling and living your best life is a lie."

The way to the truth is to examine those ideas, uncover those fake beliefs, and move through them until you find beliefs that lift your spirit and your energy.

BREAKING THE CHAIN OF BAD BELIEFS

If you've built your life around thoughts that make you feel happy and propel you to take inspired action while wearing a pair of comfortable but oh-so-classy shoes and grinning widely, then you go, girl. This is what it's about.

But, for most of us, life includes a pile of dirty laundry sitting in the bad belief corner. Usually, it's out of sight, buried under the clean stuff, or hidden behind a closet door, but filled just the same with stinky, smelly items that clutter up our emotional space. By identifying and cutting your limiting beliefs, you are pulling your power sources—the mind, body, spirit (heart)—back together. From that unified place, you can build the beliefs that will carry you toward your authentic self and your real purpose in life. Or at least you'll make a run at it and feel happy and peaceful in the process. One thing is sure, empowering beliefs will make it a whole lot easier to get out of bed in the morning.

FOUR STEPS TO UNPLUG FROM DRAINING BELIEFS

You don't have to rework *everything* to get your life moving in the direction you most want to go. Look at all the places where things are going well and you'll probably see some positive beliefs directing the flow. Our goal here is to find those that aren't supporting you, and get rid of them ASAP.

Step 1. Find What Isn't Working. Enter a conversation with your Ego.

The first step to powering up your life is to identify the beliefs that you're wired with. You could do what I do and approach this phase with determination and sheer panic. After all, discovering what is really behind your moods and behavior is a little like getting naked in front of the mirror—it's that vulnerable and that scary. But after the initial panic, this process of vetting the bad beliefs is such a relief. It's like cleaning out that closet you've had on your To Do list. It's an illuminating act of discovery.

So draw from your courage and get to work. Look at the things you do and your feelings about them. Then figure out what's behind that feeling.

Why do you hate speaking up in class? Why do you say "yes" when you mean "no?" Why do you spend money you don't have? Why do you eat so much? How does it make you feel?

When you become aware of what you're doing and why, you start uncovering those limiting beliefs. Maybe you realize that you are using food to ease bad feelings that come from not feeling good about yourself. Perhaps you're reluctant to speak up because you believe you're not very smart.

As you get closer to your core beliefs, the Ego becomes, well, an egomaniac. It starts demanding attention. Our beliefs are often so deep and so enduring that we think they are actually intrinsic to our personality. Anytime we try to rid ourselves of one of them, the Ego freaks out. "Who will you be without this belief?" our inner voice shouts. And since the answer isn't always clear, the practical mind steps in to save us from ourselves by blocking our attempts at change.

"You know," my inspired self says serenely, "I'm happy with my body. I don't need to be a size four to be beautiful. I'm going to stop dieting."

"What?" shrieks the Ego. "Girl, you're sounding a little

crazy now. Are you implying that a size 12 is okay with you? Have you seen the pretty girls on T.V.? They are *not* a size 12."

"As long as I'm healthy and active, I'm comfortable with my body weight," your best self explains.

"Yeah, right," says the Ego, "I mean you've got to be on a diet. You're not lovable or sexy unless you lose weight. Now get to it."

And so it goes. If you hear any of those little voices saying, "It is true," "There is nothing you can do," "You can't change that," or "What will others say?" when you begin exploring and challenging your beliefs, those are the messages from your mind trying to protect the Ego. This is also when you hear the Yeah-Buts:

"Yeah, but don't make trouble, you're lucky to have a job right now."

"Yeah, but there are no good men out there so you had better stick with what you have."

"Yeah, but it is so hard to lose weight, there's no way you can do it."

If you're experiencing any of these feelings or other doubts—that's a good sign. It means you are getting close to the beliefs that are zapping your energy. You're uncovering the ideas that are holding you back.

Follow the energy and emotion. Another way to identify the bad beliefs is to follow the feeling. Sherri did this to uncover a belief about work that was catching her up and holding her back from what she wanted most.

She had a high-powered human relations job at a non-profit. It came with a sizable paycheck and plenty of pressure. But she loved the work—until her son was born.

Then the challenging job outside of the home left her feeling guilty and stressed. Parenting and working full-time is draining for anyone, but Sherri noticed the exhaustion she felt during the week evaporated on the weekends. She slept better, and felt more connected to her son, happier, and more creative (she even took up stenciling). The guilt returned when she left for work Monday morning. For a while, Sherri believed that the demands of a newborn were just wiping her out, but soon she realized she felt more than tired. She felt empty. Trapped.

"I couldn't just walk off the job," Sherri says. "I liked it. I wanted to earn some money and I don't like to quit—anything. I wasn't even sure that I wanted to be a stay-at-home mom. I believed I was a career woman and that didn't match up with my beliefs about what a stay-at-home mom was supposed to do."

But the more she thought about it, the more she understood that these beliefs were just arbitrary rules that she'd had since childhood, thoughts that she'd never stopped thinking. In the past they'd worked for her, but now they were holding her back from her purpose.

After several months spent conversing with those inner

voices, Sherri quit the conversation and her job. The transition wasn't easy. She struggled with the day-to-day routine while shaping new beliefs about who she was and how her family would operate. Now, though, nearly ten years later, she says deciding to stay at home with her son was one of the best decisions she's ever made.

And, she's in the belief-busting business again. Now that her kids are older, she's adopting some new thoughts about how she can work from home and still make her family a top priority. Today, she's a certified holistic health coach, who works while the kids are in school.

Look at your life. What are you doing now that leaves you feeling tired, lethargic, and apathetic? What drains your energy without ever filling you up? Where do you feel stifled, sad, irritated, frustrated, and impatient? Those low-energy spots are the places built on beliefs that are outdated or no longer working.

Shut off the self-talk saboteurs. The language we use to talk to ourselves, those inner voices, often hold the most obvious clues to our limiting beliefs. Any vague statement, anything abstract or absolute, any phrase we use to judge or disparage ourselves, are broken beliefs talking. They are never true. They are never helpful.

Do any of these lines sound familiar?

I don't have time.

I could never afford that.

I am getting just what I deserve.

I would be happy if my husband/boss/friend/children treated me better.

I'd like to do more, but I'm _____(fill in the blank with what fits—too old, too fat, too dumb, too whatever) to make changes now.

Pain is a part of life. I just have to deal with it.

This is the way things are. I'm just unlucky.

Bad things always happen to me.

I can't follow my dreams. I need to take care of my family.

I have so much already it's selfish to ask for more.

You aren't a good person if you are interested in money and material things.

I've got to do it because the teacher told me to.

If any of these statements (or the billions of others we use) resonate with you, stop and take a closer look at it. Where does it come from? What meaning does it hold? Is it true? Can you replace it with something better?

POWER UP:

Follow the energy. If you're feeling slow, lazy, tired, if you're feeling anything but good, then your beliefs are not in support of the authentic you. Those bad feelings are a clue to long buried limiting beliefs.

Go to what isn't working. Take a look, too, at the areas of your life that aren't on track with your dreams. Look at what's not working and discover the bummer beliefs lurking behind the scenes.

Do you dream of having a loving, mutually supportive relationship, but you're stuck in the sack with a deadbeat who doesn't respect you or your goals? Hmm, chances are you have some barrier beliefs about relationships.

Do you dream of working in a career that is both prosperous and fulfilling, but you find yourself toiling in a nine-to-fiver that offers little inspiration and a paycheck that barely covers your costs? Check out your beliefs about success, prosperity, and work.

As you start to meander through this minefield of the mind, take out a pen and paper and jot some notes. Write down the truth about your relationship or job or health, as it is today then write down your dreams or goals about those things. If they don't match up, you can start unburying the beliefs that aren't working.

IN THE MOMENT PRACTICE:
FLIPPING THE SWITCH

If you hardly have a minute to spare, try this in the shower or while cooking dinner. It takes two minutes, and can be done anywhere. No supplies needed.

Think about a limiting belief you hold.

Imagine it with a physical face and body.

Name it and really feel this presence.

Treat this belief as though it is a sweet lover you're breaking up with.

Imagine yourself gently telling this belief that you no longer need it. You're moving on. Done. Adios. Buh-Bye.

Kiss it goodbye. Physically imagine yourself doing this.

Now see yourself standing alone in a white spotlight, smiling.

In that spotlight, you're going to pick a new belief, one that supports you and outshines the light you're standing in.

Imagine this belief showing up like a bachelor on the Dating Game. You question it, see how well it feels, fits, and looks. Then decide to go for a first date.

Say the new belief out loud. If it feels good, keep it.

Live from it awhile.

Then laugh at how goofy all this is. But this kind of visualization with words and pictures is powerful. It

> etches a memory in your mind and subconscious. The memory is one of expansion and freedom.

Step 2. Scrutinize the belief.

Now sort through the beliefs you've identified and keep what works.

Some beliefs really are worth hanging on to. I'm all for believing that one person can make a difference, that it never hurts to be kind, and that one glass (or so) of red wine isn't all that bad for us. But I don't go much for the beliefs that girls can't call boys, or that money is everything, or that you can't wear white before Memorial Day.

To figure out which of your beliefs are working and which aren't, say them out loud. This will help you feel the energy shift between those that serve your highest good and those that hold you back.

Try it. Say, "I am a loving person with a lot to contribute to the world."

Now say, "I'm too dumb to make a difference."

One of these feels expansive and lighter, whether you believe it or not. The other is a downer. It's constrictive. It spells doom to the spirit. That's how a bugger belief takes hold. We hear it in our heads and tighten up, become smaller, and create a smaller world around it. You don't have to do this anymore.

Choose one of your own beliefs now. Say it out loud. If it feels constrictive, we're going to question it. What we're going for are those beliefs that leave you feeling better, more expansive.

Cross-examining that inner voice. Repeat the belief that sucks the energy right out of you again. Do you feel it? Are you feeling tense or sad? Good. You've got it. Now, let's test it.

Is it helpful?

Does this belief motivate you to do better?

Does it make you feel good?

These are not trick questions and you will not be graded. If you answer "no" to any one of these questions, you're on to something. Keep going and answer the next three.

Is this belief true?

Are you sure?

Does believing this thought get you closer to your goals, dreams, and desires? Does it connect you to your greatest self?

Teacher and author Byron Katie pioneered this kind of thought scrutiny in the teachings she calls simply "The Work." The point is to illuminate our thoughts so that we can live a more grounded life from a place of truth and clarity. With this clarity comes peace, energy, and freedom, according to Katie. Our suffering ends when we realize that all along we've believed things that are not true.

If you can say "yes" to every question above, then you're good to go. Your beliefs are fueling your dreams and moving you into the flow with your greatest potential. But if a little doubt sneaks in or you answer with a big loud "no," then take a deep breath and know that now you get to do it differently.

No need to beat yourself up or live from the "I-can't-believe-I-did-that" place of regret. It is just time to change your mind and clean out those old beliefs, like closets of old clothes you know you'll never wear again.

Step 3. Catch and Release. Cutting the negative crap.

A couple of years ago, my husband was told there were going to be "major" cutbacks at work. Hundreds would be laid off. I began to worry. Then obsess. Then create a whole dramatic story around what might happen.

It went like this: Mr. J would lose his job. I would have to cook more since we wouldn't be able to afford Chinese take-out. Then we would burn through our savings, my daughter would be forced to quit preschool and ballet, and, therefore, she would have no friends at all, ever again. She would hate me for this and spend her teenage years in juvie. Of course, I wouldn't have time to worry about her because I'd be working twenty hours a day, which would cause an end to the marriage. He would get the car, and I'd be forced to walk in the snow, uphill, both ways.

Right. Didn't happen. Not one part of it. But these kinds of scary stories come from our beliefs, too, the beliefs that we're not good enough or strong enough. The idea that bad things are bound to happen, because somehow we don't deserve it so good. We play these negative thought patterns over and over. Stewing. Ruminating. Worrying. Until we decide to put it out of our mind. But as soon we decide *not* to think about something, those thoughts run us over.

"Our brain must continually remember what it's supposed to forget," says psychology professor Steven Hayes, who studies obsessive thinking and is renowned for his work with Acceptance and Commitment Therapy.

This causes the negative thoughts to keep cycling through until we begin obsessing about them. Then they become toxic and detrimental to our bodies and brains. To short-circuit their power, Hayes says, we must shine a light on them.

Start by replaying the bad memory or the negative thought or bad belief and observe how you feel about it. Treat yourself with compassion. Don't judge. Just notice the thought and let it be. And then go on with your life. When the thought comes up again, repeat the process, catch it, look at it, and let it go.

Hayes equates this process to driving a car with raucous passengers in the backseat. You notice the noise, in this case, your worries and concerns, but you keep your focus on the road ahead.

Step 4. Reshape and Reboot Your Beliefs.

Once you notice what you're thinking, also notice what is true about those thoughts and how that can serve you.

If, after scrutinizing your beliefs you realize that you are seventy-five pounds overweight, then your belief that you are fat is probably accurate. But there is nothing to support the scaffolding we so often build up around our beliefs. For example, if you believe you are fat, you don't necessarily have to believe that you are unattractive, lazy, or unlovable simply because you sit at a certain weight.

We get caught up on this. Instead of basing our beliefs on truth we embellish them, we expand the lie until they become the very trap we're trying to get out of.

How motivating is that? How will the belief that you are lazy and fat motivate you, energize you, free you up to take care of your body and lose weight? It won't. Instead you'll create a whole slew of actions—and a pantry full of chocolate and potato chips—geared to making that belief true. What if, instead of creating actions to support your bad belief, you replaced the belief with a better one, and lived from that place? It's easier than you think.

PERENNIAL PRACTICE: REBOOTING YOUR BELIEF

If you have twenty minutes to spare while you're waiting for the bus to bring the kids or when you're standing around until that chicken is done, try this exercise to quickly shift into a more positive belief pattern.

Pick one limiting belief.

Rewrite the belief. Stop the editorializing. Opinions don't matter here. Get specific. Clear. And state what is in a way that is concise and true. On some level, the belief must feel true in order for you and your Ego to adopt it. But you can have truth without judgment.

"I will never have enough money" transforms to "Right now I don't have as much money as I'd like."

"I'm fat and ugly" becomes "I am seventy-five pounds heavier than I'd like to be."

"I'm not smart enough" turns into "There are things I need to learn to be qualified for the job."

Reflect it back. This is the biggie. This is where the practice pays off. You've already transformed the belief into a clearer, truer statement, now hold it up and see what it could be. See what it looks like when it's turned around and reflected back.

"I'm seventy-five pounds heavier than I'd like to be" is reflected back as "I can make choices that nourish my mind and body."

> This is also a true statement. Look, if you are reading this book, you are making a choice to nourish your mind.

By declaring your reflected belief, your conscious *and* subconscious kick in to make it real by propelling you to take actions to validate the new thought. Soon, you'll be passing on the macaroni and cheese and going with the whole wheat penne tossed in organic tomato sauce, simply because you changed your mind.

"I don't have as much money as I would like," reflected back looks like "I am grateful for all that I do have in my life." Or, "I will now notice new business opportunities coming my way."

This isn't about punishing or making things up. It's about taking back your power and choosing to see the same thing a new way.

Right now, *right now*, you can choose to bounce the light off the belief that says you are "unlovable" and reflect it back as "I am a loving and lovable person."

That is *also* a reflection of you. It is, without a doubt, true. How do I know? Because you can always choose to be loving, and when you do so, that quality alone makes you lovable. It's irrefutable and doesn't it just feel better?

When writing your reflecting belief, stay in the present, stay in the positive, and keep it real. There are dozens of ways to look at every picture, situation, and belief. Make sure you're choosing the one that uplifts and inspires you instead of the one that keeps you trapped.

Crack Yourself Up. Go ahead, have a little fun. It never hurts to laugh a little—at yourself, at the absurdity of life. Seriously. Think about it. You are not fat just because you no longer fit into a size 6, nor do you have money simply because you own a credit card. Look at the excuses and beliefs you've been using—and those that have been using you—and have a good laugh. We can change our minds. Don't take yourself—or anyone else—too seriously. Using humor to diffuse the gravity of a limiting belief is a good way to illuminate it and let it go.

Try Out the Belief. When you've illuminated the Big Bad Belief and replaced it with one that feels better, make a note of it. Etch it into your psyche, write it down on a card, and say it out loud and silently. Live with it.

Each day, take one conscious action (your subconscious is already at work on this), in support of that better belief. Soon you'll create a habit of positive behaviors that reflect the life you want.

POWER UP:

Intuitive, teacher, and author Sonia Choquette talks about the importance of finding a set of believing eyes; someone who has faith in you and your dream that can shore you up when you are filled with doubt. Believing eyes can be provided by a teacher, partner, child, friend; anyone who reminds you of your essence and potential. Start by serving as a pair of believing eyes for someone else.

Catch Yourself in the Act. Now here's the disclaimer: en route to establishing and living from your new set of empowering and inspiring beliefs, you're bound to fall back to the old way of thinking, at least once, or a billion times.

That's okay. After all, beliefs are just a thought pattern—a habit—and on occasion we may revert back to our old ones. When this happens, stop. Take a breath. Then congratulate yourself for noticing that you slipped back into your old beliefs. That takes awareness. And reinvest in your new, more empowering thought.

As you continue to catch and replace the bad beliefs this way, they will lose their power and simply fade away.

ONE PATH:
BUILDING BETTER BELIEFS

"What does this mean?" Paige Campbell asked her husband, after she'd finished reading the letter he'd written. "What is this?"

"I want a divorce," he said.

My sister believed marriage was a forever kind of commitment and the news that her husband wanted out left her shaken and sick to her stomach. She knew he'd been unhappy—they'd talked about his mood swings and abruptness. Each time he assured her it had nothing to do with the relationship. But in the weeks and months that followed his announcement, he implied the breakdown of the marriage was all her fault and reinforced that belief by grumbling and nitpicking about everything she did.

She wasn't a good dancer, she wasn't a good cook, she was too controlling, and not attractive enough. She was the problem, he told her. He wanted a perfect relationship and she didn't fit his picture of perfect.

For a while, Paige bought into those beliefs. "I remember thinking that at one time he'd been madly in love with me," says the Portland, Oregon, advertising executive. "And yet now, I was not good enough to be loved, even for the sake of our child. I remember thinking it was something I'd done, not him." As she eased through the pain of divorce, though, Paige began to

examine those beliefs. Through serious personal contemplation, counseling, and coaching, Paige, forty, began to understand that she was actually the one who
created those beliefs about herself. When her ex said
something that caused her personal doubt, her own belief system would kick in, offering evidence to reinforce
his statements.

"I realized that I had created all those beliefs around
that behavior," Paige says. "And it was really hard and
really painful to see that the negative things he was saying were close to some of the beliefs I held deep inside
myself, for years. But once I knew that, I knew I could
be the one to change them."

Systematically over the course of two years, Paige
began exploring and changing her core beliefs. When
things came up that made her feel bad or caused her
to question herself, she challenged those beliefs, scruti-
nized them and in the process uncovered their lies. Then
she created beliefs she could own completely.

When she was feeling unworthy or unlovable, Paige
focused instead on her belief that she was a "caring person" and she looked for evidence to support that. When
she was feeling inept or unable, she reminded herself
that she had kept her house, was a leader at work, and
managed fine after the divorce. Those details were evidence that she was not inept, but strong and capable.
Each time a limiting belief poked its way in she uncovered the falsehoods and replaced it with her truth.

There were good days and bad days in this process. Replacing the limiting beliefs did not end her pain, but over time she became more aware of her own thoughts.

"I gathered enough tools to consciously walk through all that pain. I took baby steps, but I got to a better place."

Now five years later, Paige is the owner of an advertising agency. She says she is living a more authentic life now and one that is more satisfying and interesting than ever before.

Exploring, uncovering, and replacing her limiting beliefs, though, is a process.

"What I know now is that every limiting belief is from the past—it doesn't have to be my life now. I look at the belief, I draw on the truths that are opposite, those that are supportive and encouraging and powerful, and then I move on from there."

Chapter 5:

Feeling Good About Bad Emotions

The walls we build around us to keep sadness out
also keep out the joy.

—JIM ROHN

The melanoma on my knee was no bigger than a peppercorn, but the doctors described it as a "deadly form of skin cancer" and I needed surgery to determine whether it had spread. If my lymph nodes were clear, so was I. If cancer was found in them, well then, interferon and a bunch of hope would be required to heal my body. I had the surgery. Then I had two weeks to wait for the results. It was an interesting two weeks.

I wasn't afraid, though plenty of people were afraid for me, and sent me links to scary malignant mole monster websites to underscore their concern (so not helpful). The mole was already gone, cut out that first day by the doctor, so I figured the cancer was gone too. My thoughts—when I had them— were on good health.

Most of the time, I was just trying to keep up with work deadlines and my nine-month-old daughter. I had just enough time in the day to get her fed and dressed and napped and make the calls and write the articles and pay the bills and clean the cat litter. I didn't have time to worry or think about the what-ifs.

Until 3:21, Thursday morning.

I woke up sweaty, but chilled. My body felt tight. I couldn't breathe. There was a weight on my chest and in my head and what felt like a plug deep down in my throat that made it hard to swallow. My thoughts—all of them—focused on my sickness and death and what people would say about me at the funeral and how this death thing was going to screw up my whole life. I was petrified all the way through.

It took all the energy I had (and there wasn't much at 3 a.m. with a baby in the house) just to breathe. Just to push my breath down my throat and into my lungs and back out again was exhausting. It felt as though I had to will my heart to beat. It lurched and lugged in my chest. Please beat. Please breathe. Breathe again. Beat heart, please.

My daughter is so little, what will she do without me? My husband made jerky last time he tried to cook a round steak. Oh my God, what will they eat? How is this cancer thing going to work? I don't want to die. These thoughts clicked around my brain like pennies in a dryer, loud and distracting and irrational and loaded with enough ammo to keep me scared and sad and lonely.

The physical pain was potent too. It started in my chest. Sharp shooting pains, snaking through my arms and into my gut. I began crying big fat messy girl tears that ran out of my eyes and back up my nose and into my ears.

After a few minutes of this, the pain and tension still pressing against my heart, I came to realize that A.) I was not, in fact, dying in that moment, and B.) I was, I think, experiencing a panic attack.

And, suddenly, instead of fear, I felt fascinated.

I'd written articles about stress and anxiety and I have seen the shows about people debilitated by paralyzing anxiety attacks. But I'd never experienced one nor had I really experienced any deep-seated fear in my life. Sure, there's been plenty of anxiety and nervousness. But the emotions that came with standing on the edge of a cliff or having a baby (felt like almost the same thing), or starting a business and taking on other big life changes were things that I could work with, manage, move through. Never before had I felt so alone and so immobilized by fear, so at the whim of circumstance.

Now, in the middle of this Scary Melanoma Night, there was nothing to do. I was adrift, panicked, and scared out of my mind. But when I became aware of that, when I noticed all that emotion, the experience changed my life.

> **POWER UP:**
>
> Negative emotions provide contrast. When we recognize the pain, we also have a chance to experience greater joy.

I'm not saying the panic attack was fun. Nor am I suggesting you should go right on out and let your scary obsessive thoughts hijack your brain until you create your own middle-of-the-night freak-out. There are better ways to manage stress. What I am saying, is that usually when the big emotions show up in our lives, they have something to teach us if only we pay attention. Thing is, most of us don't.

THE UPSIDE OF FEELING DOWN

Many of us are on this How-To-Be-Happy bandwagon. I'm all for happiness, but there's something to be said for those funky feeling days too. In fact, the less popular emotions, like

anger, sadness, loneliness, boredom, frustration, disappointment, can fuel positive changes and build resilience. Pain is
motivating. We are compelled to move out of it. In the process,
it offers us clues about where we are and directs us toward
where we want to be.

From my anxiety-filled night, for example, I learned a little
about what others experience. I became more compassionate,
grateful, and aware.

Jessica Riesenbeck, of Houston, Ohio, felt plenty scared
and angry when the company's new owner cut her benefits at
work. But those bad feelings helped her get clear about what
she wanted most in life—security for her family—and that set
her on a life-changing path for the better.

THE POWER OF CONTRAST

Too often in this Age of Distraction we find ways to suppress,
ignore, and avoid our uncomfortable feelings. We log on, turn
on, tune out with Facebook and iPads and iPods and Blackberries and reality television and trips to the mall. We do anything
to move from our discomfort to something that feels better
without even stopping to examine why we're feeling bad in the
first place.

To constantly shift from bad to better, without noticing what is behind the emotion to begin with, is to limit your
life experience, jeopardize your potential, and totally annoy

your friends. Often the habits and behaviors we use to distract ourselves also keep us from being genuine and authentic. Sometimes they lead us to addiction and other mind-numbing behaviors that end up hurting us further and dragging down those around us. Then, aside from our bad feelings, we also have our bad behavior to deal with.

When you cut yourself off from the difficult feelings, you become trapped in an image of the ideal and you spend more time projecting and doing and spending and avoiding than being present and engaged in what is. You stay clueless and disconnected from real life—the harmony and disharmony—and it becomes harder to hear your spirit speak, says Judith Wright, author and personal development expert. Ultimately, by suppressing your bad feelings, you mute your experience of the good ones too.

The power of emotions is in the contrast. You cannot see light, without recognizing the darkness. There is no music without the space between notes. No happiness, without sadness. It's only when you are brave and bold enough to experience the negative that you are also free to experience the beauty and power of love and peace and joy.

Only by feeling bad, can you really know how to feel good.

EMOTIONS OFFER INSIGHT

When you make room for whatever it is you are feeling—even if it's fear or rage or confusion—and look on them with curiosity and awareness, then those powerful feelings can be useful, illuminating, and even motivating.

"That's why I don't like to call them 'negative,' because emotions are all good even if they don't 'feel' good," Wright says. "They have vast information and wisdom to guide us."

It isn't always comfortable. It is easier, some days, to distract ourselves, to make a Target run, or eat the ice cream, instead of sitting still with our big feelings. If you can recognize what it is you are feeling, though, before you begin dulling the discomfort, then you can choose behaviors and activities that will elevate your entire experience. In this way, emotions become a source of information and inspiration rather than a punishment to avoid.

POWER UP:

Our emotions function as an alert system. Our good feelings remind us when we are on track and living close to spirit and our bad feelings are a flare of emotion urging us to pay attention and move in a different direction.

Once I understood that my middle-of-the-night panic attack had something more to offer—compassion, knowledge—than just night sweats and stress, I became curious. The fear couldn't overwhelm me anymore. It became just an aspect of an experience I'd never had before.

IN THE MOMENT PRACTICE: COLORING YOUR EMOTIONS

When you can identify what you are feeling, you can use the emotion to guide you. Is that really anger you're feeling, or hurt? Is that anxiety or excitement?

Emotions tell us when we're living close to our values and in alignment with spirit. To tap into this power, practice becoming truly aware of what you are feeling. Use this exercise to help.

1. If my day were a color, what color would it be?

2. How does that color make me feel?

3. What does that feeling do to my body? Are my shoulders tight? Do I have a headache, or do my muscles feel loose and my stomach calm?

Then just let that color or emotion wash over you. Pay attention to the experience. For example, if your day is black and cloudy and you feel teary and tired, let the blackness wash over you and notice that it's not sweeping you away. Recognize that the tears won't harm you. There is nothing wrong, nothing to fix, nothing to judge, and nothing to do—except notice.

When we are overrun by powerful feelings, both the good kind, like romantic love, and the kind that shake us to our core, like grief, we have a hard time describing what we are feeling. Colors often invoke emotion. If you can find one that fits your mood, you get closer to understanding what feeling is working in your day (or in the moment).

HOW TO USE THE POWER OF EMOTION

Emotions are your own personal guidance system. They are energy. It's the judgment you assign to them that causes trouble or pain. What if you viewed emotions only as a tool, a source of data and information? This way, even the bad ones can feel better.

If you're feeling bored, or impatient, for example, those feelings could be telling you that you've strayed too far from your passions or values. Are you quick to snap in anger? Maybe the hostility is hiding a hurt you need to heal before moving forward. Uncomfortable feelings reveal us to ourselves, this is healing and enlightening, whether you like it or not.

PERENNIAL PRACTICE:
CHARTING THE COURSE

Pour a cup of tea, or light a scented candle, move to the Adirondack chair on the back porch, or settle in to some other serene place. Then pull out your journal for this twenty-minute exercise.

Think of one thing in your life that isn't working. Maybe your relationship is lacking intimacy, perhaps your work is boring, or you're feeling a spiritual disconnect.

For five minutes write about the trouble spot. Just jot notes.

Evaluate your notes and circle any of the feeling words or emotions that show up.

If no emotions showed up at all, what are you resisting? Write *that* down.

Assess the emotional words. Which tend toward inspiring, exhilarating, energizing? Which are more constrictive, narrow, fearful?

List out the negative emotions you've expressed.

Explore the meaning behind those feelings. If you put "bored" on the list, uncover exactly why that emotion appears in the dimension of life you're exploring. What would it take for you not to be bored? If you expressed sadness, get curious about what is prompting that feeling. Get specific.

Now, for three minutes, just let the emotion wash over you. Sit still, feel it. Notice that you're still standing.

Then consider what needs to happen to ease the bad feeling. For example, if you're exploring your relationship and you realize you feel lonely in your marriage, what would help you to feel less lonely? It's okay to feel the loneliness, but you don't have to be lonely forever. Use your understanding of this emotion to push you into a better feeling direction.

Write down one thing that you could do that would create a slightly better feeling than the one you have now.

Bad-feeling emotions are there not to hold you back or make you miserable but to help you recognize where you are, so you can make choices that will move you back into harmony with the Universe.

BEHAVING WELL DESPITE THE BAD FEELINGS

When we're experiencing bad feelings, when we are hurting, it's easy to lash out, blame others, act badly, and make a bigger mess out of everything, or as my Mom used to say, "to make mountains out of molehills."

Use your emotions for personal insight, not as an excuse to trash others or yourself. You can feel badly without behaving badly. You can feel badly without having a bad life.

When the big, bad emotions rise up, be still. You don't have to take any action at all in the beginning. Step back from them a bit and just notice and acknowledge.

Here's how it works: Say a souped-up minivan cuts you off on the freeway. Before you nestle up next to their rear bumper and give them the finger, take a breath and notice what you're feeling and get curious about why that kind of behavior bugs you so much to begin with.

This can be a bit tricky. For many of us, it's easier to go straight into a stream of profanity while smacking around the steering wheel. But then we learn nothing and the bad feelings persist and they hijack how we experience the rest of the day.

I'm not saying you have to fake what you feel. No way do you need to put on a happy face if you're ticked, but if you are aware of what it is you are feeling, you're less likely to be overcome by it. You can use the emotion rather than be controlled by it.

Maybe it's just me, but I don't naturally fall into this awareness-coupled-with-restraint behavior. When I'm feeling angry or hurt I'm not all that enlightened. Some days, I slip rather quickly into the I-am-so-mad-I-want-to-rip-off-your-head category. Even when I'm very clear about what I'm feeling, I'm equally clear that I want someone to pay for that bad feeling. This comes out in all sorts of ways around our household and I'm certain my husband could provide a complete list that includes: criticism, micromanaging, withdrawal, and let's not forget the sarcastic-toss-of-the-head "whatever" approach.

These behaviors can lead to random arguments about laundry, who had the remote last, or checkbook errors, because sometimes we mistakenly believe it's easier to push the blame on others rather than being open and vulnerable and honest by saying, "I am feeling so hurt right now" or "I'm really afraid."

When we use bad behavior to deal with our bad feelings, it becomes just another way of avoiding our emotional truth. Then we become caught in our avoidance pattern and lose a shot at all the wisdom and possibility those feelings can provide.

When you see your bad behaviors—the sarcasm, the silence—creeping into your interactions, that is a good time to step away and take a look at what is at the core of those behaviors. Then you can work with your feelings and move back into harmony with your spirit and maybe even the others in your household.

MOVING IN AND OUT OF BAD FEELINGS

This is an active process and it absolutely gets easier with practice. Fully experiencing all your emotions isn't about sitting around on the couch feeling awful for the next six months, or ruminating for days on end about how bad you feel and why. Wallowing is not awareness. I'm all for well-managed whining though. If you're feeling bad, it's okay to share and feel that.

My friend Kyle says that he gives himself time to grovel when he's feeling low, because he knows that he will soon start to feel better. It can't get any worse, right?

When things feel especially tough for me, I allow ten minutes to fuss. I might rant in my journal, or call and whine to a friend, or let my brain tell me some tale of woe—for about ten minutes. Then it's time to observe the emotion and move with it and out of it. The process is fluid.

If you think you should just keep on truckin' and avoid thinking those frightening or worrisome thoughts, that's not gonna work either. Psychologist Steven Hayes says that our efforts to stop thinking about those bad thoughts or feelings generally cause them to get stronger, more painful. We become more obsessive, more worried, and separate from our present and real circumstances. Then we fall into that cognitive loop replaying those scary thoughts and bad feelings over and over, giving energy to something that isn't necessarily true in the first place.

This is how "I am so stressed that I missed the meeting at work" turns into "My boss hates me and I'm sure I'll lose my job."

But if you become aware of your feelings—fear, embarrassment, frustration—you can pause the 8-track of obsessive thoughts and reach for something that seems a bit more sane and feels a whole lot better. This is a healthier, more productive place to be.

FIVE WAYS TO MOVE THROUGH THE MUCK

1. Identify the Misery Stabilizers.

The process of transitioning out of the bad feeling and into a better-feeling place starts when you discover what author and therapist Terry Real calls your misery stabilizers. These are the things—the nightly glass of wine, your obsession with reality television, the constant web surfing—that you do to get out of the pain, without ever really dealing with it. They seem harmless at first, but in little ways they leech the energy from your life.

Here's how it works: You're in a stressful job that you don't enjoy. To numb the pain, instead of using it for guidance, you get in the habit of drinking a couple of glasses of wine each night after work (or gossiping on Facebook or buying shoes) to manage the misery of your awful job. The nightly habit keeps you close to the couch. Instead of reaching out to friends or participating in a healthy activity, or researching other job possibilities, you find short-term relief in the wine, but the long-term pain continues, because you've done little to change the circumstance behind it.

Anytime you substitute mind-numbing behaviors for more enriching, purposeful things in your life, you are lopping off a piece of your own power. Personal development expert Judith Wright calls these "soft addictions" and we use them to try to fill some of the hollow in our lives. It never works.

2. Release Those Bad Habits.

Once you see clearly what you are doing—substituting misery stabilizers for more meaningful actions—and once you can identify just exactly what those niggling habits are, you are free to let them go. Then you can move through the muck of bad feelings toward your better-feeling nature, the one that parks right next to spirit.

It's okay to cut these bad habits back slowly, but the plan is to get rid of these limiting buggers altogether. Maybe the first week, you'll cut out the wine on three of the five nights. Perhaps you'll only Facebook for an hour, instead of the five you've been logging on for each day.

You're bound to feel a bit of pain or discomfort in the beginning. The emotions that you've buffered with the soft addictions will show up again. But this time you know they are coming. You can invite them in, acknowledge them, glean all the wisdom they offer, and then move toward something that feels better.

3. Mind Your Thoughts.

Of course your brain will try to talk you out of this by rationalizing the shopping and web surfing and wine drinking and television watching as important ways to "relax" and "unwind." These are stalling tactics and they are a good way to keep you separated from your spirit and authentic nature. Notice them, dispute them (check out Chapter Four on beliefs for some thoughts on how to do this), and move on without buying into the mind games. Then, when you do decide to surf the web, or go on a shopping spree, it will be a conscious choice rather than something you are dependent on. That's a whole lot more fun.

If you still can't get out from under your worries or negative thoughts and concerns, Hayes suggests that you take a quick time-out for a little self-talk. Take a minute to describe the experience: "Right now I'm just criticizing myself," or "I'm thinking only of what I've done wrong." And use that as way to see what really happened, instead of the story you created around it.

If the obsessive thoughts persist, try this corny approach recommended by Hayes. I'm telling you, from experience, that it works: Try repeating the obsessive thought aloud in slow motion, or in the voice of a cartoon character, or take on the tone of your mother-in-law (just to be clear, these are not the same things). By having fun with this, you're diffusing the power of the negative thought by showing it's nothing more than a bad mental habit.

4. Do Something Else.

Now it's time to fill in the space vacated by those misery stabilizers with something that fuels your soul. Take an art class. Learn an instrument. Join a cooking club. Take your husband on a date, or join a gym and exercise. Find something that moves you closer to your values, something that excites you and connects you to your spirit, and you're bound to feel better.

5. Make the Change to Move Beyond the Misery.

As you fill your life with more satisfying alternatives, step back and take a look at the origin of those bad feelings. If your job remains a source of soul-sucking drama, it's time to do something about that. If your relationship has left you feeling empty, then determine what needs to happen to help you feel less alone. There is plenty you can do—both within and outside—of any circumstance to influence positive change. It's time to take one little step. Only you know what step that is.

When you begin to move toward the moment of change, chances are you'll get a tiny emotional hit, a feeling that is a bit more positive than the one you've been experiencing. For example, you might feel your emotions shift from anger to something like boredom, or from fear to curiosity. This is your emotional guidance system giving you a little relief.

When you use this process to experience and understand your emotions, you will find that you'll spend less time feeling bad and more time feeling good, even during the daily dramas.

THE PLUS SIDE OF POSITIVE FEELINGS

Research has shown, about a zillion times, that positive feelings are a good thing. They can boost our immune function, lower our blood pressure, help our heart, ease our stress, pull our weeds, clean our house, and whip up the evening meal. Okay, not really on the last three, but the other perks are true for sure.

One study from the Group Health Research Institute even indicates that boosting your mood can help you lose weight. Depressed women who reported better feelings after a combined counseling-weight loss program lost twice as much weight as those who didn't experience any mood improvement.

While there are lots of ways to feel better—exercise, yoga, prayer, purposeful activities, healthy diet, social interaction, contemplating positive thoughts, meditation—living with our bad feelings is part of this too. It's counterintuitive, I know, but without feeling bad we would never be able to distinguish the good. And when we feel good, when we feel that spark of love or joy or peace, we are standing in our potential.

Life is not about feeling bad, it's about noticing whatever it is you *are* feeling and working with *that* to live authentically. You may not always like what you notice and you definitely won't want to go through it all, but get over yourself and get going. This is not wasted time. All this pain and crap and anxiety is motivating. It's illuminating, if you're paying attention. When you do, you see that life resides in all of these moments—the ones that feel good and the ones that don't. Nothing is void, static, or empty. Nothing is meaningless and it's all a seed of compassion.

ONE PATH:
FEELING IT ALL

For years, Himavat Ishaya, sixty-two, was wrapped up in anger, denial, and fear.

The child of an alcoholic mother, he blamed her for his challenges and he smoked marijuana and drank alcohol every day for twenty years to disconnect from the pain.

But, in 1988, Himavat says, he was "given the gift of desperation."

On the verge of what felt like a nervous breakdown and wrapped up in anger and pain, Himavat knew he couldn't continue on like he was. Instead of avoiding and denying the realities of his life, he decided to take an honest look at them. He began attending Narcotics Anonymous meetings and learned to embrace the emotions behind his behaviors. And, instead of dulling them with pot or circumventing them with anger, he stepped into them fully.

"I was so desperate and scared," says Himavat, a teacher, healer, and reflexologist, who lives in Cincinnati. "I started the process of being honest about everything in my life, especially myself. It was hard to do at first. It took years to stabilize myself and stop the habits of lying and other addictive behavior."

But he continued the work. He surrounded himself with supportive and encouraging people, attended N. A. meetings, and, for a while, worked with a psychotherapist.

"I kept looking for ways to express my feelings, so that I could get to the hurt below the anger."

At first Himavat said he was afraid he'd be overcome by the raw, unexplored emotions. His mind convinced him that the anger was too big, that he'd be swallowed up by it and unable to cope.

"But that's just the story the Ego tells," he says. "It's not true. It is never true. What I realized is that when I sat with my feelings and experienced them within my-self, and found constructive, appropriate ways to ex-press them, they moved—I mean they were gone."

Even so, Himavat sometimes still experiences anger and other hard feelings. Instead of lashing out though, he pauses long enough to become aware and clear about what's happening and then he takes several deep, lung-clearing breaths, to oxygenate his brain and ease the fear that the anger often veils.

Now instead of blaming others and holding them ac-countable for his pain, Himavat says he is "committed to living from a place of truth, compassion, non-judg-ment—it's an imperfect ongoing process," he says, but one that he continues to learn about and practice.

"I learned a long time ago that within our most trou-bling challenges lie our biggest opportunities. For a long time, I didn't believe that. I thought it was an interest-ing concept, but not one that was true. Now I know it is the truth. We can learn from all of it."

Chapter 6:

Connecting with Self-Compassion

If you don't love yourself, you cannot love others.
You will not be able to love others.
If you have no compassion for yourself, then you
are not able of developing compassion for others.

— THE DALAI LAMA

I was pretty sure the sudden flash of light *wasn't* my car entering warp speed. Though apparently, based on the numbers clocked by photo radar, I was darn near close.

When the speeding ticket crossed my desk a week later with a fine attached I was irritated at myself. How could I be so stupid? What was I thinking about? Obviously I wasn't thinking about my driving. How could I do this?

It may surprise you to find out that none of the stupid-head accusations or self-directed slander helped me to feel any better. Nor did they cause the ticket to miraculously disappear because the traffic enforcement gods saw that I was remorseful, repentant, and broke.

The mental pummeling did, though, cause me to feel pretty bad. I was down on myself all day. I wasn't all that productive, or friendly for that matter, because I couldn't stop thinking about my Big Fat Expensive Mistake. No matter how good this self-flogging approach sounds, it is *not* what I'm recommending in these pages. There is a better way, a kinder, softer, gentler approach to living, and one that makes a whole lot more sense, one that is now part of my practice of imperfection, too.

WHAT IS SELF-COMPASSION?

Self-compassion is the act of being kind to yourself even when you're feeling bad after a blunder. It's about recognizing that all of our experiences—even those that are painful and uncomfortable and involve citations from law-enforcement—are part of being alive and being human. With self-compassion you can be aware and present to the discomfort that comes with your failure or embarrassment, but it keeps you from losing perspective. After all, I got a speeding ticket, but it's unlikely my face will end up on a "Most Wanted" poster anytime soon (so don't worry, Mom). It won't hurt to cut myself some slack, and it might just help me do better next time.

Self-compassion is the bedrock for dozens of other qualities that enhance or contribute to our happiness and well-being, according to Kristin Neff, an associate professor of human development at the University of Texas, who literally wrote the book on the topic.

It's different than self-esteem in that it requires no judgment, no comparison. With self-esteem the focus is on feeling good about yourself, but it's based more on how well you do something, Neff says. That requires you to make constant evaluations and comparisons. Thing is, you'll find plenty of times when you aren't doing so well. Then your self-esteem takes a hit.

This is where self-compassion kicks in. It's a way of relating emotionally to yourself with patience and kindness, instead of judgment.

"It recognizes that we are changeable human beings with good days and bad days. That we are imperfect," Neff says. "It takes away that damaging expectation of perfection."

With self-compassion you can relax a little. Openly engage in life, and tap into your reserves of self-kindness and appreciation. This causes your brain to do the happy dance on a natural chemical concoction of the feel-good hormone oxytocin while reducing the cortisol which races through your body when you're stressed and emotionally beating yourself up.

With all that oxytocin pulsing through our bodies, we feel inspired to take better care of ourselves, and others.

IN THE MOMENT PRACTICE:
YOU'RE NOT ALONE

Next time you drop the coffee filter filled with grounds (been there), or you back into that parking post, or you pop off at your husband, or eat that bag of chips, even though you weren't hungry (done that), pause and take a deep breath and remind yourself that nobody's perfect. You are part of the human race and all the opportunities and idiosyncrasies that includes. Messes big and small are part of life and the one thing we can all relate to.

With that awareness take a "compassion break," Neff says. By repeating a mantra or phrase as a reminder to be more self-compassionate, you'll develop a habit of self-care that helps during difficulties.

Try something like, "I'm going to be kind to myself," or "I made a mistake and I'm going to support myself to get through it."

Neff compares self-compassion to the kindness and patience we levy toward our child when she struggles to read or learn her numbers. We generally don't motivate her by replaying all her mistakes, comparing her to smarter kids, or insulting her hair. We scoop her up, remind her that everyone makes mistakes, and let her know we're proud she's working hard. We reassure her that she'll get better with practice, and then we have her try again.

Self-compassion is like that. It can be strident and firm—it isn't about shirking responsibility—but it is also loving and supportive and encouraging. That can motivate us to make important changes.

The opposite is true for those who rely on self-criticism. Research indicates that that approach actually limits motivation. How could it not? When we feel bad about ourselves, we become self-absorbed and whiney and even a little pathetic. We take on the "oh-what-does-it-matter?" attitude that ensures we'll quit or continue to make poor choices and flog ourselves over them. Our productivity and creativity take a hit. And we aren't all that fun to live with.

> ## POWER UP:
>
> Self-criticism thwarts motivation. Self-compassion boosts happiness, optimism, curiosity, conscientiousness, *and* motivation.

BARRIERS TO SELF-COMPASSION

Often self-criticism is our default pattern. We believe that by being hard on ourselves, we'll become better. This thinking is wired into our belief system by a culture that isn't all that forgiving.

Cultural Ideals: Society reinforces the belief that "good" people do for others first. We grow up thinking that others are our first priority and more important than our own self-interests. So, while we may be very supportive and compassionate of others, we don't practice that kindness with ourselves.

Self-Indulgence: If you do decide to treat yourself better, chances are you'll think this is an undisciplined, lazy, self-indulgent way to go. Historically, we've been taught that if we lay back, go easy, we're simply not applying ourselves. Kindness, though, is not self-indulgence; it's care. When you get this, you'll understand the power of self-compassion.

Self-Criticism: Criticism is the Type A cousin to self-indulgence and another barrier to self-compassion. Just as you've been taught self-indulgence is bad, you may also believe it takes a stern, demanding, kick-ass, screamer kind of coach to get good results, to push you to your potential. If you go with this train of thought, you could argue that being a bully is better than being supportive. It's just not true. Over-the-top self-criticism is demeaning, stifling, and unproductive.

Constructive feedback and appropriate criticism from others can be helpful. It helps you see where things went wrong so that you can do better next time around; repeatedly beating yourself up or allowing others to attack your character, though, not so much.

That kind of unforgiving reaction keeps us close to our fight-or-flight response and shoots stress hormones—best used for outrunning lions—through our bodies. Since most of us aren't living with the King of Beasts we get all hyped up and stressed out with no place to go. So the battle rages internally. When we criticize ourselves we become both the attacker and the attacked and end up hurting and exhausted.

So not smart.

We would never teach our children to hurl insults at a friend who forgot their multiplication tables, so why do we do it to ourselves? Let's change it right now—today.

Today, we can step into our strength, and personal power. Today, we can learn to live easier with our mistakes and to develop a habit that is both empowering and inspiring—the habit of self-compassion.

POWER UP:

Self-compassion prompts feelings of safety and security, which makes it easier to admit mistakes and take responsibility for them.

PERSONAL ASSESSMENT:
HOW DO YOU ACT WHEN TIMES ARE TOUGH?

How self-compassionate are you? Take this quiz to find out. Please read each statement, and then answer yes or no.

1. When I fail at something important to me, I become consumed by feelings of inadequacy.
2. I try to be understanding and patient toward those aspects of my personality that I don't like.
3. When something painful happens, I try to take a balanced view of the situation.
4. When I'm feeling down, I tend to feel like most other people are probably happier than I am.
5. I try to see my failings as part of the human condition.
6. When I'm going through a very hard time, I give myself the caring and tenderness I need.
7. When something upsets me, I try to keep my emotions in balance.

8. When I fail at something that's important to me, I tend to feel alone in my failure.

9. When I'm feeling down, I tend to obsess and fixate on everything that's wrong.

10. When I feel inadequate in some way, I try to remind myself that feelings of inadequacy are shared by most people.

11. I'm disapproving and judgmental about my own flaws and inadequacies.

12. I'm intolerant and impatient toward those aspects of my personality I don't like.

A. Make a note of the answers you recorded to questions 2, 3, 5, 6, 7, 10—these are indicators of self-compassion. If you filled in these blanks with a lot of yeses, you probably tend to be kind to yourself even when things aren't going your way.

B. If you maxed out the affirmatives for questions 1, 4, 8, 9, 11, 12, you're probably one to beat yourself up over the quiz answers and anything else you feel that you don't get right. Try cutting yourself some slack. Look for ways to appreciate your efforts and errors instead of coming down so hard on yourself and you'll live a healthier, happier life.

(Questions reprinted with permission from Kristin Neff and self-compassion.org.)

STEPS FOR SELF-COMPASSION

Self-compassion allows you to meet life with an open-heartedness, and a tolerance that allows you to fully enjoy your successes and better manage the mistakes. It doesn't eliminate the pain, or change the reality of the experience, but it helps you move through it easier.

Next time "The Worst" happens, invoke your powers of self-compassion with these steps:

1. Admit what happened and how you feel about it. Acknowledge the severity of the offense.
2. Understand why it happened. What are the things that caused these circumstances?
3. Acknowledge the mistake. Don't judge it, just see your responsibility in it.
4. Accept your humanness. Making a mistake doesn't mean you're a bad person who does everything wrong. It means that in that moment, that one single instance, you messed it up. Now you'll fit in with the rest of us.

Here's how it works: Say you missed a work deadline. That's a pretty serious offense in my business. Not only did you not plan your time well but you kept others waiting and held up the project. You feel embarrassed and disappointed and all that is heavy to carry around. But don't smack yourself upside the head; be proactive and patient with yourself. Take a moment to look at what went wrong. Perhaps you overcommitted. Acknowledge your error. Note what you can do to keep it from happening again, and then accept your humanity. Heck, we all blow it once in a while.

Not only does this process feel better, it frees you up to do better. When we start judging ourselves harshly, we get caught up in the bad feelings and have a hard time accurately identifying what went wrong. We're apt to repeat our mistakes. Self-compassion allows you to take care of the situation and your own emotional needs without crumbling under the pressure and pain of it all.

"This way, you are able to take more responsibility for past mistakes and at the same time be less distressed about them," Neff says, "because you know it's okay to be imperfect and you don't have all these expectations of yourself to be otherwise."

This breeds self-reliance. You become less dependent on your husband or partner or mother, or the others in your life to boost your Ego and take care of your emotional needs when things go haywire. You are also more confident that you can cope with future setbacks, so you are willing to saddle up and try again. Self-compassionate people tend to be "productive people who accomplish their goals more often and behave more responsibly," according to research by psychology professor and researcher Mark Leary.

To ramp up your own reserves of self-compassion then, you could channel Stuart Smalley and repeat, "I'm good enough. I'm smart enough. And doggone it, people like me," or you could use the tips below.

THREE TIPS FOR PRACTICING SELF-COMPASSION

1. Notice self-talk. Stop and write down verbatim what those inner voices are saying. Often we're unconscious to what we say to ourselves, yet the words and sentiment can be damaging. To break this cycle of self-sabotage have a heart-to-heart with those inner voices and get clear on what you're saying to yourself.

2. Cultivate kindness. We're good at doing this for others. We take a casserole over when the baby is born, we fill in for a friend when she can't make the meeting, and we are quick to encourage others. Now give a bit back to yourself. Each day do three things consciously to nurture your body and soul.

3. Respond to every single negative emotion with compassion. You're not going to turn into some slacker if you lighten up a bit. Imagine what you would say to a friend who blows it, then say it to yourself.

Instead of "That was a dumb suggestion I made at the management meeting," go with something a little less bitchy and a bit more benevolent like, "Oh well, honey, yes, I'm talking to you; I know you were working hard to come up with a good solution to that problem. We all have moments where we say less-than-perfect things. Don't worry about it. Something better is bound to come when you have a little more time to think."

Oh, and one more thing, don't slam yourself for not being self-compassionate enough. Seriously. I know how you work—I do it too. Self-compassion is a skill to be learned. With practice, you'll get better at it.

IN THE MOMENT PRACTICE: GIVE YOURSELF A HUG

I know this technique sounds a little corny so I took it for a test drive and guess what? It works.

Find a quiet place to be alone and give yourself five minutes of kindness.

Start by putting your hands over your heart and feeling it beating. Gently lay your palms along your cheeks, wrap your arms around yourself, like a hug, or massage your neck, rub your arm.

Physical touch can release oxytocin that helps kick in our caregiving tendency, which means that when "You start acting kindly, feelings of true warmth and caring will eventually follow," Neff says.

THE TOUGH SIDE OF SELF-COMPASSION

Being kinder to yourself doesn't mean you have to get all lovey-dovey about it. Sometimes a good dose of tough love is required, Neff says. Self-compassion can be fierce and strong. There are moments when you need to kick yourself in the butt and fully recognize and accept that indeed you were lazy, or you did do a poor job, or you were dishonest, or you acted improperly.

But it's the message and motivation behind those statements that will determine whether the blunder provides a healthy opportunity for awareness and self-growth or becomes a function of oppressive despair and self-criticism.

If you respond to your failings with a general, "I suck" statement of self-criticism—"Geez, I'm such a jerk. I'm not good enough for anyone,"—then you are not likely to be motivated or confident enough to make the changes required to avoid making the same mistake again. Instead of growing through adversity, you'll become stuck in it.

The self-compassionate soul is likely to come from a place of love and inquiry and say, "I blew it. I feel bad about what I did and I will work to do better."

Failure, for whatever reason, is pretty uncomfortable. Coming face-to-face with your flaws, downright icky. But as long as you stay focused on each specific situation, don't bury yourself in past mistakes, and stop beating yourself up for wearing legwarmers in the '80s, you will be able see patterns in your life where improvements have naturally trumped the imperfections.

Self-compassion not only allows us to grow and evolve spiritually, but it draws us closer to others. While we all share this propensity for imperfection, we can also share the power of compassion.

PERENNIAL PRACTICE: WRITING A LETTER OF SUPPORT

Pull out a pen and your journal or a piece of paper and get ready to write. Self-compassion expert Kristin Neff suggests you start by writing a letter to yourself, about yourself. Start with an issue that makes you feel inadequate, insecure, and inept.

Write about how your body feels when you think of that imperfection. Describe the specific emotions that come up when you think about it. Explain the embarrassment or disappointment. Write about how you've tried to cope, or not, with this shortcoming. Have you hidden it away, blamed others, withdrawn? Be open and honest with yourself.

When you feel like you've written enough, open to a fresh sheet of paper and begin writing again. This

time, write yourself a letter of support, despite the flaws mentioned in the last letter. Write as a friend. Tell how much you love this person, yourself. Acknowledge the shortcomings, but pay tribute to the talents as well. In the letter recognize all the things, genes, life experience, parenting, circumstances, which shaped you, though you had little control over some of them. Note the inadequacy you feel, but respond as a friend would, with understanding and support and the awareness that we all have flaws, and we are all worthy and loveable anyway. Write, too, of the admiration you have for the recipient of the letter, for their willingness to understand themselves better. Remind them, too, that they are strong enough to take on any change needed. Fill the letter with kindness and acceptance and love and compassion and unabashed desire for health and well-being.

Keep the letter in a safe place. Look at it from time to time. Recognize the compassion and caring it holds for you. Remember that it started from within. All the words, all the thoughts, all the support originated within you. You have a right and responsibility to care for yourself with kindness and self-compassion.

ONE PATH:
BECOMING WHOLE
WITH IMPERFECTION

Bonnie Matthews remembers the words of the doctor well: "If you don't do something about your weight right now, you will have to be on medication for the rest of your life."

It was scary to acknowledge, but Bonnie knew the doctor was right. As an illustrator of children's books and a graphics artist, Bonnie rarely got any physical activity. She was unhealthy, and weighed more than 250 pounds. But that wasn't the only thing holding her back.

"I didn't feel so great and I think I just had this big disconnect between who I thought I was and who I really was," says the Minneapolis woman. "I lived very numb in my skin. It wasn't working well. You can't just shut part of yourself off, and ignore it. You've got to be a whole person to live a healthy life."

But becoming whole meant Bonnie had to take an honest look at her entire life—the good and the bad. Although she was passionate about her job, there was little passion left in her seven-year relationship. She'd become complacent and stuck in a routine of work, maybe a pizza for dinner, and an evening spent watching television.

Bonnie regularly turned down offers to meet friends because she didn't feel good about herself or her body.

She passed up activities that she'd once loved, like kay-aking, because she didn't have enough energy.

"I had to hold on to the side of the bed to put my pants on because I didn't have the strength to stand on one leg to do it," Bonnie, forty-eight, says.

But slowly she was waking up to the realities of her life. After the doctor's visit, Bonnie took a gentle look at her own disappointments and failings. She explored the imperfections of her life, without hostility or blame.

"I approached it all with love and forgiveness for my-self," Bonnie says. "There was no anger or hate. Anger and hate can make you stop, love and compassion can help you take the action you need to turn it around."

She began meeting with a therapist, and started walking a few minutes a day.

She cut the pizza and other processed foods from her diet in favor of whole foods, fruits, vegetables, grains. And she began learning about herself.

There were some casualties and pain. Her long-time relationship ended, and so did some friendships. Pieces of her old life fell away. It was a challenging, uncertain time. But Bonnie found strength when she realized she could cope with the changes.

In two years she dropped 131 pounds and rediscov-ered her strengths, talents, and desires. Now Bonnie is a certified trainer. She's taken leave from her illustra-tion business to promote an organic ancient grain called freekeh for a food company, and she's shared her own story on the Dr. Oz Show. Bonnie is committed now to inspiring others to live healthier by providing support, information, and healthy recipes.

"Isn't it funny, five years ago I didn't even know what a lunge was," Bonnie laughs. "Now I want to let everyone know."

Chapter 7:

Relating to the Imperfection in Others

It is only imperfection that complains of what is imperfect. The more perfect we are the more gentle and quiet we become toward the defects of others.

—JOSEPH ADDISON

When Mr. J and I talked about getting married, I argued in full support of living in a duplex. He could have one side—the one with fishing tackle on the dining room table and the mustard-yellow recliner in front of the big screen. My side would be lined with carefully shelved books and fresh flowers and clean countertops. We could sneak back and forth when we felt like it. Everyone laughed at the idea. I laughed at the idea. But I was only half kidding. Though I grew up in the household of two happily married parents, I wasn't sure about the whole marriage thing for myself.

I like my quiet. My space. My stuff. I value order and cleanliness. I like things to go my way. Marriage, at least the way I understood it, meant a lot of times things would go *his* way. It's about sharing and compromise and commitment and trust. In other words, it is not all about me.

And there was more: I was very comfortable, happy even, living on my own. I was getting to know myself and becoming clear about what I wanted, what I needed, and how totally crazy, irrational, and self-absorbed I could be. I was learning to live with my own imperfections; I wasn't sure anyone else could.

But Mr. J had this incredible, good-natured spirit and energy about him. And I wanted a piece of that. I knew I needed that in my life.

THE ENERGY EXCHANGE

Every relationship—the one you have with your mother or best friend, the one with your spouse or grocery store checker—is based upon this kind of energy exchange, according to neuroscientist Peggy La Cerra.

This is why we are drawn to others in the first place. "Being alive is an ongoing search for energy, and relationships provide an invaluable form," La Cerra writes. Romantic relationships begin then from this place of selfishness. The other individual has something we want—energy—and when we get a piece of *that*, we feel good, cared for, revitalized, and loved.

In other words, we have an agenda from the get-go. We want a mate who brings good energy *and* one who folds the whites. This need for cooperation and care stems from our evolutionary ancestors. The cave dwellers who lived and worked together tended to last longer than those free agents who refused to wash the clamshells. Cooperation was a biggie in the cave.

These days, if we have a partner, aka "Energy Supplier," who is willing to grow, adapt, clean the house, cook, chew with his mouth closed, and tell us how great we look in those jeans—we've got a good thing going. We do not want a partner who can't find the toilet brush.

"People really want gods and goddesses," says family therapist and author Terry Real.

"We all want a free pass for our imperfections and yet we all want perfection in our mate," he says. "But we are woefully imperfect human beings. If you do find your god or goddess, what would they want with you? You'll still be imperfect."

IMPERFECTION AND DISILLUSIONMENT

When you realize sometime after the wedding that the "God" you married is actually transforming back into his human state, it's easy to become disillusioned.

We enter what Real calls the "Knowledge Without Love" phase. We know our partner never picks up the towels, or wipes off the counters. We know he gets snappy when he's stressed and it's just not cute anymore. It's not even okay; we don't like it. Not one bit. In this stage we clearly recognize each other's imperfections, but we don't have a lot of love or patience for them.

Our focus goes to our partner's failings, instead of to what we can do to support the relationship. We become a self-centered energy sucker and the relationship shifts from a unified, cooperative approach into the Janet Jackson Model of "What has he done for me laaate-ly?"

IN THE MOMENT PRACTICE: FOCUS ON FONDNESS

Often we pick and fret and worry about all that our partner isn't doing right. If you're romantically involved with a human being and not a blow-up doll, you're likely to find plenty of flaws to dwell on. But for five minutes, while you're doing the dishes, or folding the clothes or driving to work, or listening to a song that you love, focus only on the good things, the things you love about this person, the things that make you laugh. Get very specific, and as your mind starts to wander to the irritations (yeah, it will), bring it back to fondness. When we remember what we truly love or appreciate, we also act more loving. Just a few minutes of focused fondness can ease a little relationship strife and promote better feelings.

THE GAP BETWEEN REAL AND IDEAL

This process—the shift from the honeymoon phase to the you-make-me-crazy phase—can be sudden and mystifying. Though the common misconception is that opposites attract, research shows that we generally enter into relationships with people who have similar backgrounds, behaviors, and attitudes. We relate best to people who are like us. And, perfection seekers that we are, we like it when our partner represents some aspect of our ideal. When our partner, the kind and patient person who listens well while whipping up a tasty carbonara, becomes more real than ideal, it's disappointing, unsettling, and totally and completely annoying.

This makes it much easier to blame him for *all* the failures in the relationship, as well as the growing unemployment rate, and the hostility in the Middle East. When you're focused on the imperfections—especially those in others—they show up *everywhere*.

So we go to work trying to change our partner, I mean the situation, for the sake of the relationship. We do this by nagging and criticizing. We roll our eyes and respond sarcastically. We interrupt and overreact to show our displeasure, and hopefully, motivate him to knock off all his freakin' irritating behavior.

POWER UP:

When we focus on what's real rather than the ideal, we recognize that our partner's imperfections can actually strengthen the relationship, or at least make it more interesting.

Sometimes people do change or they are willing to work to improve at least some aspects of their behavior. But mostly what you get when you try to force your partner to live up to your own expectations of perfection is angry. Angry that those same old issues keep cropping up and angry that nothing is getting better. This anger leads to sadness and an emotional chasm. A spiritual disconnect occurs, too, when you live with judgment, impatience, and intolerance for others. Spirit emanates from love and compassion. It doesn't usually cast a vote on who is the better driver.

A healthier, more practical way to nurture a life-enriching relationship is to drop the self-righteousness and hypocrisy and get real about the baggage *you're* bringing into the relationship. Then you have a real shot at building a relationship that is interesting, honest, and sustainable out of all that imperfection.

"What rankles us can also unite us," Real says. "Perfect is boring. With imperfections you have the capacity to dive deeper into your own growth."

HOW IMPERFECTIONS POWER RELATION- SHIPS

The cosmic joke, then, is that the same flaw-filled moments and behaviors that drive us crazy in our relationships are essential to helping us heal, connect, and learn.

Greater Intimacy. Closeness emerges from a mutual tolerance. To be less than perfect and still be loved is a gift and one way we learn how to love others. When we 'fess up to our imperfections and take responsibility for our mistakes, we are showing respect and vulnerability to our partner.

An expression of sincere emotion can do this too. When you open up and say, "I'm afraid" or "I'm not good at this" or "I feel embarrassed," or when you offer a genuine apology and say, "I'm sorry," you are inviting your partner in.

He then can offer up empathy, support, forgiveness, or insight. He can share the moment of discomfort with you and you become allies.

POWER UP:

A sincere expression of vulnerability or weakness can inspire intimacy and passion.

"That kind of sincere sharing promotes compassion, inspiration, and creativity within couples," says relationship guru Katie Hendricks, of The Hendricks Institute and co-author, along with her husband Gay Hendricks, of *Conscious Loving: The Journey to Co-Commitment*.

Oh, and here's a tip: Don't be a jerk when your partner is sharing his vulnerabilities. This kind of disclosure can be enlightening and helpful, but if misused as a weapon during a fight, it will undermine the intimacy and trust you've established.

Greater Health and Healing. Plenty of research indicates that our mental and physical health, longevity, and well-being is influenced by our mates. If one person makes bad or unhealthy choices, the other tends to as well. When my husband opts for a milkshake, for example, I'm rarely standing at the door saying, "No, honey. That's not a smart choice." More likely, I'll give him a quick kiss, hand him the keys to the car, and push him out the door while yelling, "Make mine chocolate!"

But romantic relationships do contribute to healthier habits as well, and can help heal old wounds.

Real and other family therapists and psychologists like Harville Hendrix, PhD, say we are unconsciously attracted to people who we believe will satisfy the emotional needs that we didn't get met in childhood. Real calls it our "unfinished business."

Often, he says, we choose to be in relationships with people who are a milder version of our parents or childhood caregivers. These people then inadvertently help us recreate our early challenges so that we can, with any luck, master them, move beyond them, and finally grow up.

"The imperfections then become a resource for our own

healing," Real says. "Our imperfections harken back to childhood and the relationship can become a Petri dish that can help
grow a new you."

Greater Self-Knowledge. Another way our partner's flaws benefit us is through greater self-understanding. Think about this:
If there is something that really bugs you about him, you probably do it too. The things we are able to see in others are often
the things we need to work on within ourselves.

Instead of lashing out then, next time he procrastinates,
let his annoying behavior teach you something about yourself.
Then get up and clean out that closet you've been meaning to
get to for the last two years.

Part of being in relationship is about picking the person
with the issues that you can live with, issues that match up
best against *your* issues. If you can remember that your mate's
imperfections aren't manifest simply to make you batty, you'll
do better. And, no matter what *he* says, your flaws do not make
you the devil incarnate.

Instead of getting hung up on every little thing, lighten up
a bit. Laugh together a little more. Let a few things go and offer
up some compassion and forgiveness to each other. That can
make day-to-day marriage management a whole lot easier.

RELATIONSHIP TIPS AND TABOOS

Taboo: Making it Personal

The other day, my husband, Mr. J, parked so close to the rock wall in our driveway that I couldn't open the door. Fortunately, aided by my squealing (think puppy locked in a car with the windows rolled up squealing), he quickly noticed his error and moved the car so I could actually get out of the vehicle, thus ending the drama. Or so he thought.

It was not over for me. "How could you do that? I mean, why would you park there so I couldn't get out?"

"I guess I just wasn't thinking," he said.

"*What*! What? I am your wife, how could you *not* be thinking of me? Did you forget I was sitting there? I gave birth to your child, for goodness sake, and you can't bother to make room for me to get out of the car? *I* am always thinking of *you*," I huffed.

Except perhaps in that moment, when I was thinking mostly about how ticked I was. We ended up spinning into an argument about how I overreact and he's self-absorbed. It was not a good night, but we did have a quiet dinner.

What if I hadn't taken it all so personally?

We all do stupid things. Mistakes happen. But everything that comes up is not a statement of your value to the relationship. It is not always about you.

Tip: Offer Compassion

"The Dalai Lama says that being compassionate is the one time when it's okay to be selfish," says Dr. James Doty, director of The Center for the Study of Compassion and Altruism Research and Education. "Because when you are compassionate to others, you also benefit so greatly by doing it."

When you give to someone else, when you offer kindness and compassion, not only does the recipient feel better but your own stress levels decrease and you become more nurturing. All this is good for the relationship. With compassion you step into what Peggy La Cerra calls "enlightened self-interest." In other words, you give a little, you get a little, it's all good.

Taboo: Expecting Too Much

When I got married, a wise friend of mine told me, "Don't expect him to fulfill your every need. He can't do it all. He doesn't have to do it all. Give to yourself and find family and friends and others to give you some of the things he cannot."

That's good advice for any relationship. We are multidimensional beings with varied interests and desires and no spouse or mother, or partner or girlfriend can fill all the roles in our lives, and they don't have to.

Your spouse's inability to pick upholstery colors, for example, isn't a shortcoming or failure. His apathy when it comes to the green moldy stuff in the fridge isn't anyone's fault. Differences—while at times hard to live with—don't have to be a liability.

Tip: Remember the Alternative

When you are caught up in the niggling annoyances of a relationship, consider the alternative, says self-help and relationship guru Arielle Ford. What would it take to forever eliminate the muddy shoes in the doorway or the wet towels on the carpet? Probably the end of the relationship or the demise of your significant other. This is a bone-jarring alternative.

We all have little habits and traits that are probably not going to change—ever. Mr. J pours out his pockets on the counter each day and it makes me crazy. But when I realized that to have clean counters would mean I no longer had Mr. J, things got really clear. I'll take a cluttered counter any day, as long as I have him in my life.

Tip: Stop Keeping Score

I used to be a scorekeeper—silently weighing how much I do during the day compared to how much he does. I decided to change that bad habit when I realized one night that he takes out the garbage, every single night, without complaint. He just does it. I've found that by appreciating what he does do, instead of making comparisons, I feel better and we're more cooperative.

Same is true with arguments. Our disagreements basically fall under two categories: parenting and communication, with a little give-me-the-remote thrown in. But we know that both of us have made a bunch of mistakes over the years, so it's not even worth keeping track. There are no grudges here. We're doing our best, and sometimes even that is terrible. But if you both continuously throw out gold stars or red checks every time someone does something, your relationship becomes more performance-based than a partnership. That way, somebody is bound to lose and that is bad for both of you.

Taboo: Looking for Balance

No matter how much effort you put in it's never going to be equal so get over it. There is no such thing as balance in life or in love. There are entire weeks where I'm making the meals and doing the laundry and the bulk of other chores while he's immersed in work or on a special fishing trip or whatever it is that is attracting his attention. And then life will tilt back a bit and he'll step in and do more than his share when I'm out with the girls or consumed by work, or whatever it is that's driving me that week. We go like this, back and forth. Sometimes totally engaged and working together, other times half-zoned out with the partner picking up the slack.

It is not a perfect process. Relationships are rarely a slew of equal moments shared 50/50 but ultimately it all evens out.

Everyone gets a shift. The key is to keep talking about what's important to each of you and the relationship, to expand and constrict around the needs of each individual, and then to find time to regroup as a couple.

Tip: Watch Your Words

Choosing your words carefully when you're talking over problems, imperfections, or daily dilemmas can make the process more productive. If something is bugging you, it's definitely worth talking about, but phrase it as a question or request rather than as a complaint or criticism.

Here's how it works: You feel angry and overwhelmed by the amount of responsibility you're taking on at home. Instead of launching into a "you-never-do-anything" monologue, start the conversation differently.

"I'm feeling tired and overwhelmed and it feels important to me to have some help around the house. Would you be willing to do the dishes tonight?"

By making a request you invite your partner into the process. It allows you to state your needs and gives him an opportunity to meet them without feeling criticized or nagged. You may not get the answer you want, but hopefully, it will be the start of a respectful conversation.

Other words like "thoughtful" and "understand" have been shown in research to help diffuse arguments and lower stress. "I statements," where you begin with "I" and then express how you're feeling or what you need, also work to put your focus solidly on yourself and to share your experience without blame.

"Often, during an argument or disagreement, we slip into our territorial or reptilian brains and experience the fight-or-flight emotions and behaviors that leave us feeling defensive and combative," Katie Hendricks says. A careful choice of words can eliminate that edgy feeling, connect you to your cognitive brain, and help you communicate effectively to solve problems.

"The big payoff is that you spend less and less time in repetitive patterns that never seem to resolve the big issue," Hendricks says.

Tip: Take Time-Outs and Give Do-Overs

My friend Kelly is good about giving do-overs and she reminds me of the importance of making space for screwups.

Sometimes we just get it wrong. We don't do it on purpose. We're human and we make mistakes. In these moments remember that not everything has to be a life lesson. Not everything needs to be talked about or understood or explained or apologized for. Not everything means doom to the relationship. Sometimes, a mistake is just a mistake.

This is the prime time for a do-over. When someone—as in you—veers wildly off course into anger or blame or over-reaction, take a deep breath and ask for a do-over. Make sure you offer plenty to your partner too. Most of us do a lot better when we get a second chance.

Or, try a time-out. Don't just huff out of the room, but mention that you need a break and ask if you can finish the conversation when things have calmed. Then go someplace quiet, take some deep breaths, clear your head, and come back to deal with the situation in a less confrontational way. I even do this with my daughter. Sometimes instead of giving her one, I offer a time-out to myself, and then I run like crazy for the bedroom. A pause can help you move from the big emotion to a more productive problem-solving perspective.

Tip: Forgive

Even the good among us think about the merits of revenge. Anthropologists say it's a universal trait to want to go after those who came after you. In other cultures, revenge worked to deter those who might do future harm. In intimate relationships, it doesn't work so well.

Forgiveness, another evolutionary quality, is a better way to go. Research out of Stanford University indicates that those who cannot forgive, experience greater stress and health problems including heart disease, cancer, high blood pressure, and lower immune response. Hanging onto the stress of what happened can actually make you sick. Forgiveness is the antidote.

Tip: Give a Good Hug

Hugs, handshakes, and even high-fives have been shown in studies to boost performance and promote healing. Another study indicated that students who received a touch on the back from a teacher were twice as likely to participate in class, says Tiffany Field, the director of the Touch Research Institute at the University of Miami School of Medicine.

Touch unleashes a physical and emotional response that reduces stress, eases dark moods, and helps us feel better. Lack of touch has been associated with more aggressive and violent behaviors.

Make time for this kind of physical connection with your partner. Hold hands. Reach over and pat his arm, or gently place your hand along her cheek. Give a shoulder rub. Hug him when he walks through the door. Physical contact is a basic human need. Make sure you are reaching out, in a literal way, to each other.

IN THE MOMENT PRACTICE:
MAKE CONTACT

Next time your partner walks in the door, get up, greet him with a hug or a kiss, and hold tight for a minute. This isn't a sensuous, let's-get-it-on kind of touch, just a tight, loving, nurturing embrace that's good for both of you.

Tip: Take Care of Yourself

There comes a time in every relationship where you need to take a clear-headed look at what's going on and ask, "Am I getting enough from this relationship to make what I'm not getting okay?"

Obviously, violence in a relationship, or abuse of any kind, is a deal breaker. Seek professional help, call a domestic violence hotline, and learn how to get out of the situation in a way that won't put you at greater risk.

AN ACT OF FAITH

Every union has a unique set of challenges and issues and imperfections that ebb and flow with the happenings and circumstances of our daily lives. To be deeply connected to one another is to live gracefully with your partner's imperfections, as well as your own. This can be hard to do, but when we work at it, we also have a shot at knowing ourselves better. We get a chance to love and be loved and the freedom that comes from that. It's all an act of faith, for sure, but that is the spark of all spiritual growth.

PERENNIAL PRACTICE:
A MOMENT OF APPRECIATION

Turn the television off, put down the iPad and the iPod and the iPhone, and sit down and talk to your partner for twenty minutes.

Start by sharing five things you appreciate about him, preferably specific things you experienced that day. Perhaps he checked in from work, or did the dishes, or gave a good hug, or picked up the kids from childcare.

Don't ask or expect him to share his appreciations with you. If he does, great, but this is your gift of love and compassion to him. It also helps you see that despite all of the imperfections there is plenty of good going on in the relationship.

This practice, particularly if you do it daily, or at least several times a week, helps you connect to that goodness.

ONE PATH:
A FOCUS ON WHAT WORKS

His sarcasm makes her crazy—and makes her laugh.

The way she gets so emotionally wrapped up in things bugs him a bit, but he loves how caring and compassionate she is.

Despite twenty years together, thirteen of them married, and the changes and challenges that come in any relationship, Kristin and Josh Mauer say they focus more on what works than the irritants and imperfections in the relationship.

"There have been times when I'd try to change her or she me but I don't think that would ever work out. I don't think we really want to do that," says Josh, thirty-seven, manager of a landscape company. "I know myself better. I know who she is and it's all okay. I think we can understand the differences and not get upset about all those little things. Everybody has their stuff—things that are negative—but we don't get too wrapped up in all that."

Five years ago, though, things weren't quite so easy. Financial challenges pushed Kristin to take a job she despised that kept her away from their two daughters. Josh's long workdays at the company he built added stress and the relationship was bowing under the pressure.

"It was just kind of a gray time," said Kristin, thirty-five. "I got to a point where I was just totally lost. I stopped doing the things I liked to do; we had financial stress, and a routine that consisted of chores and duties. It created a lot of friction. We lost our solidarity."

Instead of calling it quits (both admit they thought about it), the couple sat down, reexamined their values and their dreams for the future, and realized their marriage was part of that plan. Then they made some big life changes.

Josh sold his business and took a job in Mississippi. Kristin was reluctant to move away from both of their families, but she agreed to the change because it allowed her to be home with their daughters and together Josh and Kristin reconnected as a couple. Out of one of the most difficult times in their relationship evolved one of the best.

"There definitely are bumps in the road," Josh says. "But the big thing is what are you going to do about that? Are you gonna cut and run away or stay and make it work?"

To make it work, Kristin and Josh, who now live in Virginia, rarely focus on the other's flaws and they often move beyond disagreements by agreeing to simply let them go.

"Nobody needs to be right or wrong. It isn't about winning," Kristin says. "It's about accepting each other and the circumstances and moving on and moving toward what matters more."

"You can get pissed, but the bottom line is it's really not that big of a deal. Why hold on to it and let it flood through the rest of the day?" Kristin says.

"You can choose what to focus on," Josh says. "I think Kristin and I focus on all the good there is."

Chapter 8:

Practicing Faith, Building Optimism

The uninitiated are those who believe in nothing
except what they can grasp in their hands, and
who deny the existence of all that is invisible.

—SOCRATES

Once when I was a kid, I caught my dad standing next to
the Volvo with his head slightly bowed. It was just a second's pause, before he climbed in the car, and I asked him
what he was doing.

"I was saying a little prayer," he said, "asking God to keep
us safe."

Here was this man—a powerful and reasonable force in

our family bowing to something nobody could even see—it made me think.

We were not a church-going family, but our house was faith filled. We had faith in each other, faith in ourselves, faith in the sense that we were worthwhile as individuals, faith that we could make a difference. I had this deep knowing, too, that it wasn't all about me. There was always something bigger at work.

ACTING WITH FAITH

Faith is so personal, yet universal, that it's hard to find a word that describes it just right. Everyone has their own definition of what faith is, but it's easiest to understand by watching how faith works.

Faith is falling in love. It's raising a child. It's trying again to run the race, get the job, make the marriage work, or learn the language, when you failed the first time and the third time and the sixth time. It's understanding that all this pain and crap and mess is not without meaning. It's believing that things will be okay even when nothing feels okay. It's about being awed by the sunset though you've seen it a hundred times before and hope to see it a hundred times more. It's knowing that there is something bigger than what you can see and feel and touch and it's behaving better because of all that.

Faith is custom-made for human beings, or at least those

of us who subscribe to this practice of imperfection, because it allows for do-overs. It's not an excuse. It doesn't mean there aren't consequences for bad behavior, but it means that you'll get another chance to do better next time.

And on those days when you forgot to pack your kid's lunch and the check bounced and you're too fat for your good sweats and it's raining and the carpet needs cleaning and your computer is down at work, faith will be there, too, reminding you of what really matters.

"Faith is whatever animates you and allows you to see that things are always more than they appear to be," says Rabbi Brad Hirschfield, author and president of CLAL, The National Jewish Center for Learning and Leadership. "There are always greater possibilities around now and in the future than what reality suggests."

POWER UP:

Faith is the belief in something bigger than yourself.

It is not a religious thing, though it obviously shows up there. Faith in God can be powerfully resonant and important, but you can also have faith that the bus will show up on time, says Rev. Susan Sparks, Senior Pastor at the Madison Avenue Baptist Church. Or, that the check will come in the mail.

"I don't think faith is limited to anything," Sparks says. "It can include a higher power, if one chooses to follow a spiritual path, but you don't have to be religious to have faith."

In this way faith is a whole lot more practical than mystical.

THE PRACTICAL NATURE OF FAITH

"There are times in life," Sparks says, "where we hit a painful experience or crisis. Faith is what gives us a bit of grounding and balance to get through it. It's like finding that place in a pool where you can actually touch ground with your feet."

Because faith is intangible, it isn't limited by what we know or can conceive. It's bigger than that. Like our grandest dreams. Like love.

We raise children. We love them the best we can without really knowing the people they'll become. That's faith. We marry, not knowing how the union will go, but believing that we'll work hard enough, love big enough, to keep it together. We shift careers to pursue our passions, not knowing if it will work out, but believing it's worth a try. Faith frees us up to live this way, to love completely and dream big. Even amid the uncertainty and imperfection of all that is this life, faith is a knowingness. It's trusting that we are on the path we are supposed to be on. That better can appear from the bad. There is confidence in that, one that keeps us going.

Here's how it works: The amniocentesis indicates Down syndrome, but you continue the pregnancy. After the initial despair, you embrace this child and the pregnancy is both an exciting and scary time. When the baby is born, you don't see the Down syndrome at first, what you see is your beautiful baby and you love her immediately. Sure there are medical challenges and backbreaking expenses and raising a child with physical and mental limitations is not easy, not in any way. There are nights you cry about it and there are nights, too, when you hold your kid close thanking God for this child. And you move forward, opening up to the experience, learning what you need to know to raise your daughter, finding others to help, and never once believing it isn't worth the effort.

IN THE MOMENT PRACTICE: FINDING EVIDENCE

The next time you're running errands, pause for five minutes in the parking lot to consider all that had to happen to get you safely to that spot.

At one time you had to find the money to buy the car. Then the engine had to start. Stoplights worked, road crews kept the asphalt maintained, others drove cautiously. There are a thousand little things that had to happen just right to get you from point A to point B.

Now, I'm guessing, that you're a bit like me and have no idea how all of it came together. Probably, don't even care. I mean, come on people, just hurry it up, I need to get to the bank. Right? I know nothing about the electronic thingamajigs that trigger the stoplights. But they still work and help me get to where I need to go.

That's how faith works. It works whether you know how it happens or not. It's your job to notice.

ROOTS OF FAITH

Unconditional love—that quality that is both so simple and so hard—is the breeding ground for faith. When you can give that to a child, when you can feel that for yourself, when you know you are loved completely, faith flourishes, Hirschfield says. You learn that you are a grand and marvelous person and at the same time you know your own smallness in a vast Universe. "You feel both important and modest," Hirschfield says. That prompts you to ask:

What can I do for others?

What can I do for myself?

In this way faith is motivating. It gives us the confidence and inspiration to do, to try, and to persist.

FINDING OUR WAY

Your job then is to connect to your faith. To find that place, that part, that sits close to your core, your essence, your spirit. You can spend a lifetime looking for this kind of love and forever trying to find faith, but it's already in you—it's been there since the beginning. Perhaps you've lost sight of it a bit. Maybe it's been clouded over and covered up by bad beliefs, pain, trouble, and uncertainty. But the light is still in there and faith stems out of that.

Martha Beck substitutes the word "trust" for faith to get away from any religious dogma and beliefs that can sometimes catch people up. Faith, she says, "is the trust that this moment will take you to the place you need to go if you allow it to be as it is without any resistance whatsoever."

Think of this as spiritual aerobics. To find your faith, to live from that place, you must act as if you already have it.

You must trust in a higher source, seek out evidence of faith at work, even when things seem so screwed up. You must become brave enough to move forward, despite the doubts. You must accept what shows up and trust your intuition when it all seems illogical. Living with faith means you stop micromanaging the Universe and start experiencing it.

HOW FAITH SHOWS UP DURING THE TOUGH TIMES

This is all good when things are humming. Clients are coming your way, your husband isn't being stupid, the kids aren't sticky, and there is money in the bank. Faith is easier when life feels good, but it's necessary when things feel bad.

On September 11, 2001, I sat in front of the television watching the news broadcasts and wondering if my faith would survive that day, if it mattered anymore. When those towers collapsed and families were splintered, and our nation was shaken, I questioned what kind of so-called bigger power could let things go so far.

That day, I was assigned to write a newspaper story, for a future issue, about the Mt. Hood National Forest. After watching the news and feeling kind of hollowed out inside, I hopped in the Mazda and drove into Oregon's Cascade Range to work.

What I experienced was bigger than burning buildings. There, from deep in the woods, rose this massive mountain chiseled by snow and wind and weather. It towered into the blue sky along the edge of our Universe. And what I knew in that moment was that there were things so big, so energetically powerful and pristine, that terrorists could never take them out. What I knew is that people would go forward in love and faith to rebuild families, buildings, and lives. That we would grow from the pain because we are part of the same energy that created that mountain, this Universe. Faith doesn't mean we aren't fired up in hurt, but it's a reminder that we are enough to get through it.

It can be argued that the terrorists were acting from faith on that day, too, but I don't believe it. Faith is rooted in love, based in a belief of the highest good, not Ego, not dogma. The attacks were not an act of love, but much of what came out of them, was.

When we take those difficult moments in our lives and rebuild, start over, begin again, love anyhow, we are expressing our faith. And in those moments when you feel as though you are about to be swallowed up by despair, you've got to go looking for your faith again. Don't wait until it is dimmed by doubt. Find it, foster it, commit to it, and it will help ease you through the troubling times.

Start by paying attention, slowing down, asking questions and being open to the answers. Prayer, meditation, quiet moments in nature or in church, and journaling are other ways in.

Faith can also show up in bold and raucous ways when we tap into the energy that connects us all by connecting to each other. I've felt surges of faith, both personal and universal, when I danced with my daughter to Earth, Wind, and Fire, and when I, along with fifty thousand others, heard the National Anthem played by a college band before a football game. I've felt it when I watched a kindergarten teacher talk to her students with a smile so big I thought it would push the roof right off the building.

FAITH IS NOT FICKLE

Faith is fluid and active, but it also demands monogamy. You don't just stop living with faith the moment something doesn't go your way. It isn't a quick fix. Nor is it an antidote to pain, though it helps to handle the discomfort when you believe the crap can morph into something meaningful.

"It is a bit easier to hold onto faith when we let go of expectation," Sparks says.

When we load up our lives with the expectation that we should have all the answers, or that we are entitled to a life free of pain, or that everything should go our way, our faith becomes vulnerable.

But when you are buoyed by faith, you're able to step into the ick with the knowledge that all that is happening is propelling you to the place you need to go.

By contrast, hope is a bit more passive. It is a fervent wish, a deep desire for something to happen or for something different. That wishing becomes more active when you throw optimism and faith into the mix. Optimists believe things can get better and they're willing to work to make it happen. Faith then is the confidence, the inner knowing that propels you. It "gets you off the couch" to do what needs to be done, Hirschfield says.

ADVANTAGES OF OPTIMISM

Optimism does not mean that you feel happy every minute of the day. It doesn't mean that you're always upbeat and in a good mood. You are not even required to keep your fingers crossed so that all your problems will disappear and your glassy-eyed, smiley-faced joy will return. That's not it and it's a good thing because most of us wouldn't be able to buy in to this rosy-cheeked cheerfulness.

But optimism is doable. It is real and it can be a difference-maker in your life if you stay grounded and realistic. Grounded optimism is about attitude and action and like so many of the other strategies that manage the flow of negative emotion, it helps you feel better. It helps people bounce back from adversity and it is one component of resilience. Doctors, like positive psychology guru Martin Seligman, rank optimism right up there in line next to exercise and good nutrition when it comes to good-health building behaviors.

That's the key: optimism is a behavior, not a trait. This means, to all the pessimists out there, that you don't have to feel left out. Optimism can be learned. It's both a behavior and an attitude that can be adopted and practiced. Even if you think it won't work for you, it's worth giving it a go.

THINGS CAN GET BETTER

According to Dr. Larry Dossey and others who have studied realistic optimism, it consists of two parts: a flexible mindset and focused action. Optimists get things done. They are willing to shift, adapt, change their goal if necessary, but they keep going. They persevere because instead of being stymied by the setbacks, they deal with them. They hope for the best, know the worst is a possibility, and then they work with whatever appears.

Here's how it works: Three weeks after the job interview you find out the position has been filled, and not by you. It's a blow. You're discouraged but you're an optimist driven by faith. You know that things will work out and something better will come along. Instead of scarfing down the bag of cookies that you bought for your kid's soccer snack (or maybe after scarfing them down), you get to work calling your contacts and updating your website for potential employers. During one of those calls you connect with an old friend who tells you about an unexpected opening at the design firm where you've always wanted to work. The company needs to make a quick hire. Are you interested?

During the periods of frustration or setback, you can keep your optimism alive by actually acting optimistically. Keep busy moving toward your goals or dreams or desires. Apply for the job, sign up for a gym membership, and buy the travel magazines in preparation for your dream trip. Do something that moves you in a direction you want to go. If you do this often enough, your attitude will soon follow your actions.

POWER UP:

You don't have to always feel positive or upbeat to be optimistic. Grounded optimism is about recognizing the difficulties, believing things can get better, and then making them so.

PERSONAL ASSESSMENT:
HOW OPTIMISTIC ARE YOU?

· · · · · ·

Take this true/false pop quiz (don't worry, you're not going to fail) to figure out whether you see the glass half full or shattered into shards dribbling good wine all over the picnic table.

1. Things usually go my way.
2. I'm just unlucky.
3. A good bottle of wine and a good book are antidotes to a bad day.
4. Life is hard.
5. Opportunities usually emerge out of setbacks.
6. I expect that I can figure things out.
7. The best way to deal with a problem is to go shopping.
8. If I don't get excited, I can't be disappointed.
9. There is little I can do when things go wrong.
10. The nightly news is a real pick-me-up after a bad day.
11. With hard work I know I can meet my goals.
12. I try not to dwell too long on my problems.

Answer Key: Alright, before you settle the score, disregard answers 3, 7, 10 for being just plain goofy and irrelevant, though a good wine and a good book can solve just about any problem. Then give yourself two points for True answers to questions 1, 5, 6, 11, 12.

8 to 10 points: Your glass is more than half full of a crisp chardonnay and life is good. When things do get a bit murky, you believe you can make it better, so you work hard to improve rather than get hung up on some woe-is-me tale. This optimistic attitude will help you move through challenge and uncertainty with grace.

4 to 6 points: All is not lost, you still have some wine left in the glass and part of you knows there is another bottle in the kitchen. With a little practice and some focused action you can strengthen your optimism. Look at what is working well in your life, reach out to friends for the support you need, and reframe the trouble spots and your optimism will increase.

0 to 2 points: Uh oh. You are a pessimist. No surprise, right? You figured you would score low on the test—I mean that *always* happens. But it doesn't have to. If you want to ease off the negative mindset, follow the exercises in this chapter, and throughout the book, and you can develop your optimistic side. Acting optimistically is the first step to becoming that way.

AMP UP YOUR OPTIMISM

Of course all of this is optional. You don't have to be happier. You don't have to do things that make your world better. If you're happy being unhappy, closed off in a corner of darkness certain that the world will end or that the Starbucks on your corner will close, leaving you in a trance-like decaffeinated state, that's fine with me. But if you want to feel, say, just a teeny bit better, there are a few strategies you can try to up your optimism.

Know What You Think. "Building optimism is not a matter of thinking more optimistically, it's a matter of thinking less pessimistically," Seligman says.

So, what thoughts are you having?

Question Your Thoughts. Once you're aware of what is coming to mind, ask yourself these questions:

What is the problem or setback that's got me freaked?

What do I believe about that situation?

Are those reactions, thoughts, and beliefs true? Really?

When we are going through a tough time it's easy to get wrapped up in negative thoughts and ideas. Most of these thoughts are full-out false. Catch yourself before buying in. Undress those ideas. Examine your beliefs. If they aren't helpful, let them go and pursue another perspective.

Watch Your Language. The way you talk back to yourself can offer a clue as to whether you're primed for pessimism or able to move through the challenge optimistically.

Say you've overslept, you're having a bad hair day, *and* the car ran out of gas. What do your inner voices have to say about that?

Is your "entire day" doomed? Is "everything" going wrong? Do bad things "always" happen to you? Are you "super sick" of my annoying use of quote marks?

Pessimistic thoughts tend to cluster in sweeping generalizations that imply long-term troubles as opposed to temporary circumstances. The car stalling is downright annoying, and probably cuss-worthy, but it doesn't mean you'll end up living alone on a school bus with thirty-two cats. The bad hair day? Well, that's another story, but since you have to go out looking like that anyhow, wouldn't it be easier to watch your words and speak kindly to yourself rather than holding up your hair as a symbol of all that is wrong in your life?

Difficult things don't have to signify a downward spiral that will limit your life. Cut out the absolutes and generalizations and you're likely to shut out some of those negative inner voices as well.

Reframing the Tough Stuff. Then take a new look at the situation. The concept is relatively simple: if you change the way you see something, you can change your circumstance. You can change your life by changing the way you look at your life.

Reframing doesn't mean that you move into denial or that you ignore the negative feelings or experiences. It represents the possibility, though, that there is more than one way of looking at things. Life is rarely black and white. When things are going less than perfectly and you're in the midst of a struggle or challenge, you can hold onto a sense of joy, possibility, and curiosity even while you are feeling scared, sad, or angry.

For example, it can be true that you are feeling scared, disappointed, and guilty about your divorce. And it can also be true that the divorce creates some feelings of relief and excitement around your newfound independence and opportunity.

Reframing allows you to see the situation from all sides, and then you can focus on the one that feels more helpful, more optimistic.

When you're in the midst of trouble, it's easy to feel swallowed up by it. If you remember that life is fluid and ever-changing, you'll remember too that these problems are rarely pervasive, and they are never permanent.

The Energy of Yes. Living with faith and optimism doesn't, shouldn't, and can't happen all in your head. It's a whole mind/body/spirit thing. That means you have to get out there and live with this stuff. You have to apply it to the moments of your life.

Bad things are bound to happen, but when you let faith settle in, when you adopt the attitude that you can roll with whatever comes, you're free to live big. Have fun. Try new things. Love openly.

I was reminded of this a couple of years ago when life became a bit dull. After years of feeling like I'd taken on too much, I put more boundaries in place by saying "no" more often. I got good at it, in part thanks to the women's magazines that ran banner headlines like "Say No Now!" But after a while, life felt more predictable and routine than interesting.

So, I let the yeses back into my life. It's not like I abandoned common sense altogether. I cannot do it all, nor do I want to. Sometimes "no" is necessary and important but I think before answering now. I say "yes" more often and I've become conscious about why I'm inclined to say "no." Now, if I'm tempted to turn down an opportunity because I'm afraid, or uncertain, or insecure, I say "yes" instead and I move with faith and optimism that I'm on the right path.

IN THE MOMENT PRACTICE:
JUST SAY YES

Once today say "yes" to something unexpected that comes into your life.

Know that you are enough to handle whatever emerges from the yes. Know that you have the whole Universe supporting you. Believe that you will have a good time and learn something that you need to know. Exercise your faith by taking the Universe up on the good things that come your way and practice your optimism by believing that there is more to come. Just. Say. Yes.

Then take two minutes to reflect and answer these questions for yourself:

What did you say "yes" to today?

Were you inclined to first say "no"? Why?

How did you feel when you said "yes"?

What did you learn about yourself by saying "yes" to this thing?

What do you know now that you didn't know before you took the leap?

That simple little yes-strategy has opened up my life. I've begun talking more publicly about the things that move me, and trying new things in my career. I've reconnected with longtime friends, laughed more, and I even go out and do fun things—smack dab in the middle of the week now—gasp. I signed up for a class I didn't think I had time for, and I love it. All this yes-ness has energized me.

Jennifer McLean, author of *The Big Book of You* and host of "Healing with The Masters" teleseminar, talks about the vibrational properties of "yes." She believes that simply saying the word is expansive. It raises the energy, and sweeps you into the flow of the Universe.

When you say "yes" you are backed by faith. When you make moves in the direction you want to go, despite your fears and uncertainty, despite tough times, you are behaving optimistically. With this one-two punch of faith and optimism you align with spirit in the best and worst of times, and you live knowing that whatever shows up will be there to serve you.

PERENNIAL PRACTICE:
LOOKING BOTH WAYS

Write down three situations in your life right now that are bugging you. Perhaps you're worried about your job, or tired of your partner not unloading the dishwasher, or stressed about money, or fed up with your food cravings. Pick three things—big or small—that are sources of negative feelings.

Now reframe each situation at least once.

Get creative. There are dozens of ways to look at any one situation. By seeing a challenge from all sides you're likely to stumble across a more positive perspective that will ease your stress and guide you through it.

Each time that original stress surfaces return focus to the thought or perspective that feels more helpful. Notice how it directs your emotions and actions toward something better.

ONE PATH:
FINDING FAITH IN FICTION

It was a 2006 trip to Rwanda that started journalist Jennifer Haupt thinking about her faith in a new way. "The entire trip was a leap of faith," Jennifer says. "I went for a month to report on several stories that fell through, and wound up discovering the bones of a novel—something I never dreamed I'd be writing!"

Twelve years after the 1994 genocide that pitted neighbors against neighbors, resulting in the massacre of nearly 800,000 members of the ruling Tutsi tribe by the Hutus, Jennifer spoke with many survivors of rape and torture. Along with the remaining grief and sorrow, she was touched by the hope, compassion, and even forgiveness expressed by many Tutsi widows and orphans.

"I really saw—and learned—the meaning of grace: letting go," Jennifer says. "It takes a certain kind of faith, beyond religion, and it can be extremely healing. I started thinking about my own faith, and letting grace into my own life."

That self-exploration led Jennifer to begin work on a novel about a young woman's search for her father—and a part of herself—in post-genocide Rwanda. Jennifer spent two years diligently working on this story but when the publishing market crashed in 2008, doubts crept in about whether it was wise to continue the work.

That's where faith came into the picture.

"Faith is daring to do something, daring to believe, regardless of the consequences," Jennifer, fifty-one, says. "I kept writing every day as a show of faith, even though the desired end result—publication—wasn't guaranteed."

That doesn't mean there aren't down moments, or even days of doubt and frustration. That's when faith becomes a practice and Jennifer draws from what she calls a "Toolbox of Rituals." She does yoga and takes long walks in the woods with her dog. She gardens, and brings fresh flowers into the house. She nourishes her body with healthy, whole foods instead of giving in to the quick fix of a Ben & Jerry's splurge.

"Faith is about keeping on your path," Jennifer says. "It's all about attracting positive energy and it can't hurt to believe in something bigger than what you see in the mirror."

Chapter 9:

Creating Through Uncertainty

An essential aspect of creativity is not being afraid
to fail.

—EDWIN LAND

When my daughter was first learning to talk, I became
a faux Dr. Seuss, putting together silly words and
sounds to help her make connections and comprehend
the rhythm of language. Silly schmilly. Easy peasy. Fish spish.
Cheese schmeeze.

And something unexpected happened—I got into it. I
mean I started liking these cornball combinations and found
myself looking for interesting sounds and words even when

I wasn't entertaining the two-year-old. I even made up definitions for my made-up words, and created jingles. I played.

These silly little songs began to subtly change my day. I began playing with language and in some kind of back-end way that helped me to be more imaginative and playful during my day-job as a writer. These funny-punny rhymes sparked interesting connections and ideas, prompted me to recall old memories, and they became mental exercises that kept me engaged (don't hate me Moms out there) during the often mind-numbingly mundane routine of caring for a toddler. I don't think it was just the word play, but the habit of being silly that helped me loosen up a bit. I became more engaged, more curious.

CREATIVITY AS A SUPERPOWER

This is how creativity works. When you unleash your creative energy, or like in my case let it dribble out in tiny, immeasurable doses of goofiness, you end up looking at old things in a new way. You identify new approaches, novel ideas, and become more flexible and open-minded in the way you live your whole life.

Creativity is a good thing, too, for romantic and intimate expressions whether you want to spice up things in the sack or simply woo your partner with love notes or surprises. It's vital to protecting our most cherished relationships say researchers, like Robert Root-Bernstein.

With our imaginations we are able to step into our partners' metaphorical shoes to understand just why he's acting so stupid, I mean, why he's behaving in a particular way. It can help, too, with conflict management. If you and your partner challenge yourselves to come up with new ways of dealing with the same old argument, you might find a fun way to end the issue once and for all.

When people look for creative solutions, when they turn toward new possibilities instead of old problems, they also engage with each other in unique and meaningful ways. The ditties I created for Sweet P provided a new way to communicate and play with her. She started coming up with her own sounds and rhymes. We cracked each other up. It was fun.

Creative expression also fires up the immune system and contributes to resilience because it allows you to bend and shift and see possibilities where others see limits. Tufts University psychologist Zorana Ivcevic found after polling college students that those who acted creatively every day reported greater personal growth and well-being.

"It's a way of understanding our world," says Dr. Ben Michaelis, a clinical psychologist in New York who uses creative expression to help his clients. "It is the way we learn. We are developing human beings, we are developing souls and creativity is a part of that."

STOP WITH THE "YEAH BUTS"

Still I can hear the "yeah buts" from here. "Yeah but I'm just not a creative person." "Yeah but I'm not crafty." "Yeah but I can't draw a straight line."

Yeah but, may I remind you, that once upon a time you were pretty good at this stuff. Most of us had rampant imaginations and clever, unique fort-building skills or problem-solving strategies that helped us figure out how to stack cushions and blocks just high enough to reach the cookies on the counter without cracking our skulls.

POWER UP:

Creativity is innate and it gets stronger with use. So start playing with it again. Look for unique approaches to old problems, try a new recipe, try your hand at the arts or a craft you enjoyed as a child and feel the power of your creative spirit ignite.

Though it may have been suppressed, that creativity wasn't just sucked out of you. It's wired in. Now it's just a matter of rediscovering that energy again and making space for it, Michaelis says. That process starts with a new definition.

DEFINING CREATIVITY

A friend once told me, while she sculpted a wizard's hat from the metro section of the newspaper, that she wasn't creative at all. Another claims she has not an ounce of creativity in her body, yet you should see the notes and the rhymes she puts in her daughter's lunchbox.

It's in all of us, this ability to make something wholly original and interesting where before there was nothing at all. We are inventors. We are creators. Yet instead of honoring that essential quality most of us cling to the foreboding feeling of creative lack. It isn't that we aren't creative (though Pictionary is certainly *not* my medium), it's that our definition of creativity is too narrow for practical application in everyday life.

In ancient times both the Greeks and Romans thought creativity was something passed on to a person through mythological creatures, directly from the gods. Western religions talked of creativity as a result of "divine inspiration" or an expression of God's work.

In today's culture we tend to view creativity in terms of outcome. If we can't paint like, oh, say, Monet, we believe we are simply not creative and therefore we should give it all up.

But creativity is not about competing against others or mimicking the styles of the masters. We don't have to color in the lines. In fact striving for some version of that ever-elusive perfection can scare you into perennial procrastination, a creativity killer for sure.

Creativity is really about process and personal meaning. It's about connecting to your essence, your spirit and then allowing for something to emerge from all that. It's about working with the same energy that created the Universe to paint a bold life experience. It's not about painting, writing, sculpting, building; it's about living. That definition is broad enough to include all of us.

BIG C, LITTLE c

There are categories of creators, say the experts who study this stuff. Master artists, musicians, and writers like Michelangelo, Mozart, and Shakespeare are called the "Big C creators," according to University of Oregon associate professor Ronald Beghetto. Their ideas, their creations, shifted the way we all think about our world.

Others, the writers and dancers and painters and other so-called creative types who have actually carved a career out of the creative realm, are called "Pro C creators."

But many of us are acting out our mini-c creative tendencies when we develop "novel and personally meaningful interpretations of experiences, actions, and events," write Beghetto and James Kaufman.

And the rest of us? We *own* the Little c category. This

one belongs to the mom who constructed a wizard's hat out of newspaper, to the novel lunchbox-note writer, to the dad who crafts a wooden toy in his shop, to the Food Network wannabe who figures out how to sculpt radishes into fantastic garnishes. Anytime you've used duct tape differently, resolved a kid's tantrum in a new way (hopefully *not* with the duct tape), or figured out how to tweak a work project to fit the client's preferences, you've connected to your Little-c side.

It's not always clean or obvious. Creativity can be sloppy and disorganized. Our best ideas can seep from a series of associative leaps that make little or no sense at all, in the beginning.

The brain operates through a series of connections and associations. Every word or thought or experience or feeling triggers a series of other thoughts, connections, and associations. Even when we're focused on one thing, disparate memories pop into our minds. Or we'll glean unexpected insights to an unrelated problem. This is how my daughter shoving a raisin up her nose led to the practice of imperfect spirituality.

In a very real way one experience can cause new associations that lead to something surprising, something entirely and creatively different.

We do this all the time in conversation. We'll be talking on one point when something a friend says triggers another thought that leads the conversation in a different direction. We'll say, "That reminds me…" or "That makes me think about the time…" or "Along those lines…" and launch into another story or experience. It's organic and free-flowing and stimulating and fun. You're never sure where things will lead. At its best, associative thinking is uncertain and open-ended. For new ideas to emerge you've got to sit back and see what develops. You've got to follow the connections no matter how quirky and settle back into the uncertainty, into the unknowing, before you start seeking solutions.

We are wired to do this. Your creative powers swell out of you whether you're a kid playing pretend, a parent negotiating a positive outcome with a reticent teenager, or a person finding time for a spiritual practice despite the craziness of the day.

When you think of it like this, all of life becomes a conscious creation. But, it's "the getting it from the inside of you to the outside of you that feels hard," Michaelis says.

And that hardness can be softened when you develop a daily habit that helps you face down your fear of imperfection and allows for the creative power to surge through you.

IN THE MOMENT PRACTICE:
A NEW TWIST

Build this three-part exercise into your schedule each week. It's a way of "priming" or preparing your mind to create.

Choose a challenge you face each week. Maybe you have to come up with a new dinner menu every night, or get your son's teeth brushed without a battle, or find time to meditate in the midst of a demanding schedule.

Think about this for two minutes and then ask yourself these questions:

What needs to happen to make it easier to deal with?

What could I do to make it more fun?

What are some new things I could try to manage the situation?

What would the ideal feel like?

Keep this short. Start pondering sensible and silly solutions. You don't have to figure it all out in two minutes, just get the process started.

Now get up and go. Water the plants, go get the mail, work on a crossword. Do something else completely unrelated and let your unconscious fiddle around with the problem for another ten minutes. This promotes associative thinking. Give your mind freedom to follow its disjointed or seemingly nonsensical leaps. Be a quiet observer.

At the end of the ten, sit down with a paper and pen and write down any thoughts that come to mind with respect to the challenge you posed.

Maybe you'll have a lightbulb moment, or, maybe not. Either way, by involving your cognitive and conscious mind in the act of creation, it's likely ideas will continue to percolate until you find a new way of looking at the task. No matter what comes out of it, this simple practice, used regularly, is a good way to put you back in touch with your creative side.

IMPERFECTING CREATIVITY

The ability to come up with the innovative idea or unique product is a natural thing. Unfortunately, it's also one we naturally suppressed by the time we were about seven years old.

In the beginning, kids aren't saddled with the same societal rules or comparisons we take on as grownups. They aren't required to be experts or have all the answers, so they are free to explore and question and experiment and create as a way of understanding their world better. It's how they learn.

By the time we turn eight or nine, though, things change. We become more focused on measuring up, getting it right, making the grade, and most importantly, not looking stupid. We begin, quite literally, coloring inside the lines.

Here's where the drive for perfection gets in our way. We neaten things up, accommodate the social groundswell, become experts in our area (often because we stop doing other things), and we follow the rules. To fit in, we stunt our own creative energy.

It doesn't disappear though. Your creative power sits there, dormant, waiting to erupt, waiting to color your life with authenticity and vitality. But, before you can let it flow, you have to get comfortable with the notion of imperfection. You have to move into a place of open-mindedness, and get used to making mistakes. Creative people mess up more than anyone else, probably because they are willing to take more chances. They are brave enough to live bigger.

This approach, this openness to learning and living, is called a "beginner's mind" in Zen Buddhism. With a beginner's mind, you are open and curious, willing to question and accept and experience all that is.

"I love being a beginner again," writes Zen Master and psychotherapist Mary Jaksch. "I love following impossible instructions. I love failing gloriously."

In that failure, the creative person recognizes great potential.

"There are no setbacks here," Michaelis says. "Emotional and creative expression do not follow a straight line. What you think of as a setback is only a variation of the process."

Here's how it works: You're ready to start your own business, and while you have the drive and the determination, you are lacking the dough. In your attempts to recruit investors, you develop a presentation that doesn't yield any results. So you shape it, edit it, and do it again, but you're still not getting the money you need. You're not worried though; you just start playing around with other ideas. Everything inspires you.

You create a soundtrack and visual presentation, you give away products, and by harnessing your own imagination you capture the imaginations of others who then decide to buy in to your business.

Instead of being stymied by the failures and paralyzed by the risk, you actually used those things to find a new way to solve an old problem.

BEING BOLD WHEN THINGS GO BAD

Living a creative life, then, is a bold move. To commit to your creative powers means that you are also endorsing a practice that requires, by its very nature, failure. Creativity demands trial and error, experimentation, exploration, mess, sleepless nights, lots of coffee, and sometimes M&M eating (or is that just me?). Sometimes it also requires tolerance for the terrible, because in the beginning, the process is rough and unpolished.

Writer Anne Lamott talks about how all good writers begin with "shitty first drafts." It's a combination of the mess and imperfection that ultimately drives the development of better second drafts and good third ones.

This is true for everything in life, whether you're a computer programmer or a working parent or landscape designer. Rarely do we arrive at the "perfect process" or "ideal solution" the first time out. We learn best by blowing it. By finding out first what doesn't work.

Creative expression is dependent on some sort of silliness and uncertainty and curiosity and our bullheaded stubbornness to just keep going. It requires the courage to bulldoze through our fears of looking stupid and sometimes behaving stupidly so that we can express ourselves in a new way. In other words, the first step to creating beauty is to know what ugliness looks like. The first step to creating an innovative product is to discover what won't work.

LIVING A CREATIVE LIFE

When you create, you connect to the Divine Source and the energy that created the mountains, the oceans, cheeseburgers and chocolate, and the blackberries sweet and warm just off the vine. You tap into the same source that created marvels like honeybees and you and me and the energy that leads to love.

When you live as a creator, you hang in a place of possibility, the place where ideas flow through and around you. I've had moments where I actually felt my body charged by this current, as though I were vibrating with the energy. When you're done after a day like this, you feel utterly exhausted and exhilarated. The world is different somehow. You know something new and that's gratifying and exciting and optimistic.

Of course, I've had days, too, where I just end up grouchy and sticky with ink on my fingers, and a certainty that even a Pet Rock is a masterpiece I could never create. On these days, I do one important thing—go to bed. Then I get up and try again tomorrow. Your creative spirit will still be there for you, even on the tough days when it's a little slow to show up, because once it's been reawakened it doesn't go quietly. In fact, it can be tough to avoid. It will trickle back in, probably waking you with an idea in the middle of the night, or arising during a hot shower. It's always there for you as long as you believe, as long as you go looking for it.

POWER UP:

Part of living a creative life is to believe you can. Know that you are a creative force, aligned and connected to the creative source of all—the Universe. If you believe that, you will act from that truth.

Creativity is that powerful. It is a dynamic and evolving process. It is always risky. It is always enlightening. It is always worth it. It is a link to the power of God within you; the place where we connect to the universal energy.

It's no mistake that this chapter comes right after the one on faith, because not only is creativity inherent to spiritual alignment and expression, it requires guts and big-time faith to let flow this power that you've hidden away for so long.

But, to me, it feels far scarier and riskier *not* to make something of your life. Not to release this power of imagination and fun and potential.

A psychic once told me (when my daughter was very young and I had little time to write) that if I didn't find my way back to my work, or if I didn't soon discover another form of creative expression, I'd get sick—physically ill. She told me that creative expression was so critical to me as an individual that if I didn't let it loose the blocked energy would harm the cells of my body until some dreadful disease took over. It would, she said, probably show up on my left side since that's where creative oppression often appears. It is her belief that if we don't use our energy to create, it goes haywire within us.

I don't have a clue whether that's true. But I think about her words when I look at the four scars along my left leg where the melanoma sat. I think, too, how rarely I've been ill since I began working on this book. And how, even on the days when the writing comes hard and I hate it and I would much rather be outside in the summer sun sipping a margarita or biking with my daughter, I think that I am so much better and happier for having dipped into my soul to come up with a different way of seeing it.

STAGES OF CREATIVITY

When you are immersed in the so-called act of creating, it lays out like this:

Preparation: Something triggers an idea—you're looking for a solution to a problem, or you're tired of the routine and need a change—and your imagination takes off, fantasizing about how things could be done differently.

Incubation: These ideas, seemingly unrelated and impractical, start buzzing in your unconscious while you're chopping carrots or going for a walk or sleeping.

Illumination: All of a sudden, they gel together. Bingo. You've got it. Now you know what you need to do and you know how to do it. This is a moment of sheer relief.

Elaboration and development: And so you get to work. You actually write the book, solve the management problem, develop the plan, and express the idea. Insight moves to action, which creates something that can be shared with others.

For me, these stages are rarely this clear or definable. My stages look more like this: "The Messy Stage," followed by the

"I've Got Nothing Sheer Panic Stage," which often leads to the "Begging the Universe to Give Me Something, Anything Stage," soon to be relieved by the "Bingo, Aha Moment," which is usually replaced immediately by the "How the Heck Am I Gonna Do That?" phase.

It's like a sticky web of convoluted, adrenaline-producing ideas and rotten sentences and rejections and failed attempts and irrelevant comments and personal insecurities and days without a shower.

All of this baloney yields some great drama to share with others, but not a lot of well-developed material. Until, all of a sudden, it does. Until, from the drama and uncertainty and nothingness, there emerges something.

It seems that just when I'm about to fall over the edge creatively and I'm wholly convinced that the best I can do is finish my daughter's Cinderella coloring book, I get a flash of insight, or a good idea, or some clarity. When after all that angst something breaks loose and moves in and out in a way that feels good and makes sense, it feels like pure joy. It's exciting, and each time it happens I'm filled with awe and gratitude. It feels like magic. I don't know how the trick works, but I'm thrilled that it does.

"There are no hard, fast rules to creativity," Michaelis says. Like so many spiritual practices, the doing is what matters most. You are not going for perfection here, you are going for the experience, the engagement. You are using creativity to connect to life.

HABITS OF CREATIVE PEOPLE

This doesn't mean you sit around waiting for inspiration to strike. Creative people actively work to cultivate creativity in their lives. It's a mind/body/spirit exercise to be sure and to get it started you have to stretch, rework, and refire some of those neurons that have gotten lazy over the years. Once you begin exercising your creativity again, those nerve pathways develop in your brain to accommodate further expression. This makes it easier, and more natural to do.

Build in some of these habits practiced by people living close to the creative edge, and creativity soon becomes a way of being.

Practice empowering beliefs. Everyone is creative—yes, even you. Believe it and then find evidence to support that belief.

Create with awareness. "If you're thinking about being creative, you start to act creative," psychologist Ben Michaelis says. "If you start to do it, then it becomes a habit."

Find inspiration and passion. Seek inspiration. Fill your life with amazing books, beautiful vistas, and engaging people. Stare out the window at the trees blowing in the breeze. Put a plant in your office; a study at Texas A&M University showed employees had more ideas and flexible solutions when flowers and plants were put around the office.

Nature is like a shot of espresso to your creative drive. Pay attention; appreciate the smallest spiderweb, as well as the majesty of mountains. Use the wonder of the world to drive you toward your passions.

Poet Rick Smith II encapsulates this when he talks about his creative process. You don't have to wait for inspiration, he says, "because inspiration surrounds us everywhere we go. It is in what we see, feel, observe, or experience. It shows up in memory, dreams, people we meet, family, strangers, and so many more ways. Creativity comes from the heart and is designed to explain our reactions to observation. Life makes me feel most creative."

Work consistently. Expression is inherent to creativity. It's not enough to think it through; you've got to make something out of it. A great idea won't write the book. Flowers don't bloom unless the seeds are planted. Creativity must be worked. Sit down, go to your studio, or find a time and a place to do the work every day. Sketch out the plan, create the recipe, and practice the craft.

Embrace crapola. Even with the best idea, a lot of what you create is gonna be really, really bad. So buck up, little camper, get over yourself and move into the place where bad becomes the new good. After all, the power of creativity isn't in the outcome; it's in the process.

Have fun. Let loose a little. Laugh a lot. Try new things. Daydream. Watch clouds. Build in time for fun, for play.

Play with your thought patterns. Look at the familiar items in your life: the bag of coffee, the cheese grater, your iPod and imagine it as something else. What else could it be? How could you use it? My daughter created an ingenious wallet out of a slinky the other day.

Or take on a routine task a whole new way. Drive home along a new route. Try a new recipe, using only what's in your pantry. Experiment. Novelty makes a difference.

Step out of your creative comfort zone. When I want to create something new, I work with words, but that is not necessarily expanding my creative muscle. If I pick up a mound of Playdough, (or a pen and sketch pad, or pasta dough) I'm in a completely different creative realm: Open and able to see possibilities, willing to abandon rules for the creative desire just to see how something might turn out. It gets my neurons buzzing and happy neurons are healthy neurons. Try it. Express yourself differently today and give your brain a buzz.

IN THE MOMENT PRACTICE:
PLAYING WITH THE ROUTINE

To add a little zip to your life, start looking at the world in a different way—in made-up, silly, imaginary ways by using this exercise mentioned by Dr. Michaelis.

Next time you're running errands create a new world to explore.

Headed to the post office? Imagine what it would be like to travel through a windstorm or while driving through a field of peanut butter.

Pretend you're shopping, in an underwater grocery store. What kinds of packaging would hold up? What food would still be good, which would go soggy? How would you look in Scuba gear?

Imagine you're headed to the school, on the back of a camel—what would that look like?

What if you spoke only gibberish? How will you make the teller understand you?

Share with others. The manifestation matters just as much as the idea. It's important to share your creative impulses and productions, Michaelis says. But be thoughtful about who you share with, especially if you're just rediscovering your creative self. The right kind of support is an important part of expanding the creative process.

Settle into the void. This can be big-time scary. This is where you are brave enough to sit in a place of emptiness—after you've created—trusting that you will do so again.

Psychotherapist Julie Rudiger calls this empty space, where there is little energy left to create and not a single new idea, the "The Fertile Void." I love that, because "fertile" implies life. It reminds you that when you are uninspired or lame or lazy or vacant the creative spark isn't dead, it is only quiet. Unexpected things emerge from this fallow period. Then comes a flurry of activity and adrenaline and passion, until you're spent again.

Persist no matter what. Living creatively is a lifestyle. It is a lifelong expression of spirit. Don't paint the painting and be done. There are unlimited mediums and ideas and expressions and Little-c applications for self-discovery. Keep asking questions. Keep expressing your thoughts and ideas. Keep trying. Persist. Persevere. Adapt, change, create, and repeat.

STEPPING INTO YOUR SPACE

The very nature of creation is growth, expansion, expression. You make something new, out of nothing. I'm idealistic enough to think that all that matters. That creating makes a difference, uplifts the world, and greases the natural flow of life.

When you create, you move beyond your time and your space and swell with energy and imagination and possibility.

This kind of expansion is not always comfortable, but it's always worthwhile. It's meaningful and it can move you closer to your greatest values.

PERENNIAL PRACTICE:
PUT FUN ON YOUR TO-DO LIST

Find something you like to do and do it twenty to thirty minutes a day. Play, have fun. It's a great stress reducer, sure, but it will also boost your productivity and problem-solving abilities while fostering a flexible mindset. This makes it easier to adapt when things don't go your way.

Need a refresher? Here's how to play in two steps:

1. Pick something that you know you love to do and make time for it each week. Or, if you're no longer sure what stokes your interest, revisit something you loved as a child—stamp collecting, dancing, model building, martial arts, or photography. Keep playing with different activities until you find one that sticks.

Or find fun by taking on something new. Try something you've always wanted to try. If you enjoy journaling, now try sketching pictures alongside the text. Take a guitar lesson, or start a scrapbooking project.

2. Keep it up. Challenge yourself to learn and grow and expand your knowledge and practice of this hobby

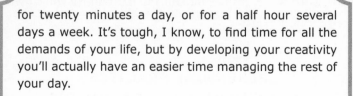

for twenty minutes a day, or for a half hour several days a week. It's tough, I know, to find time for all the demands of your life, but by developing your creativity you'll actually have an easier time managing the rest of your day.

ONE PATH:
COOKING UP CREATIVITY

Brent Mather makes a career out of designing structures, but the architect's creativity doesn't just end at the office. For the Denver, Colorado, man, every aspect of life is a creative experience.

"From business management to communication, personnel and problem solving, creativity can be part of every process," Brent, forty-one, says. Three years ago, that awareness helped to change his life.

A workaholic on the edge of burnout in 2008, Brent began meditating. He also renewed his commitment to exercise and healthy eating. He read new thought books and became aware of how each element of life and each human interaction holds the potential for creative expression.

"If there is balance then the creativity part is very easy," Brent says. "You need to be aware and present to what you're trying to accomplish and in that you set a framework that allows creativity to manifest."

"Meditation sets the framework for creativity because it allows me to see the possibilities," Brent says.

Sometimes, like in a group brainstorming session, creativity shows up not just in the ideas being bantered about, but in the way the session is run. "Creativity appears when you bring the right energy and openness and ask the right questions so that others are encouraged to share ideas," he says.

But the pockets of quiet, uninterrupted time, the mini-breaks Brent gets during the day, are what allow his own ideas to bubble up.

This is when he mulls over options and looks for ways to merge the client's desires with function, vision, and a budget. Often a thought will sit and percolate in the back of his brain until it forms into something just right for the project.

Even then, "there is always some risk involved in creating," he says. "The process is shaped by trial and error, and failure is part of it."

Clients may reject the design, the architect may hate some aspect of the solution, and it may be too expensive, but Brent says he uses that information and keeps exploring.

At home, the creative process extends to the kitchen

where Brent plays with ingredients and recipes to concoct culinary creations. Usually, it works out. He has an instinct, a flair that leads to good-tasting food, except when it came to the truffle tamale. There was some sort of chemical reaction with the ingredients and the pan that left the tamale tasting "disgusting," he laughs.

But, "you just go with it. You learn from those mistakes," Brent says, "and you just keep cooking. You keep creating. It's a way of life. I'm truly trying to make everything creative. I'm constantly failing at that but meditating or reading and exploring these things keeps me connected creatively."

Chapter 10:

Living a Value-Driven Life

To live is to choose. But to choose well, you must
know who you are and what you stand for, where
you want to go, and why you want to get there.

—KOFI ANNAN

A t the end of the day I usually settle into the brown chair
with cat scratches on the arm and open a book or jot
on the crossword. Mr. J sits across from me reading or
watching something on T.V. and I can hear my daughter talking herself to sleep in her bedroom, her soft, sleepy voice telling
stories, or singing songs about fairies and stars. On the nights
when I'm lucid and I don't have dishes to do and the grownups

aren't arguing over the wreckage of a bedtime meltdown or the destructive nature of Sponge Bob, I can feel my heart swelling with gratitude for this moment. Not only is it one of my favorite times of day, it's one of the best parts of my entire life.

This scene, as it plays out many nights, leaves me with a deep feeling of satisfaction and peace. The kind that comes when you feel as though you made a difference in the day, as though you did what mattered while fulfilling some of your own desires by living close to your values.

The experts call it "values-based happiness."

"Values-based happiness is a sense that our lives have meaning and fulfill some larger purpose," writes Steven Reiss. "It represents a spiritual source of satisfaction, stemming from our deeper purpose and values."

It's different than the feel-good form of happiness that is more reactionary and fleeting. This kind of happiness rises up when we buy a new pair of shoes, or kick ass at Scrabble, or visit with our girlfriends. Something happens—we see a funny movie, receive a check, have sex—and our response is to feel happy. When the moment passes, so does the feel-good emotion.

> **POWER UP:**
>
> Values-based happiness requires you to figure out what matters then live a life that satisfies those desires and moves you in line with your values.

Values-based happiness is sustainable and unlimited. Once we know what we value, our desires become clear, Reiss says. When we go about satisfying those desires, we move into alignment with our values and that helps us to create a life that is both meaningful and happy.

LOSING SIGHT OF WHAT YOU VALUE

But, here's the thing: I don't think a lot of people know what they truly value anymore. When was the last time you thought about it? So often we live by default. Our parents were Democrats, so we vote Democrat. Our grandfather taught us that it's necessary to work fifteen-hour days to be a good provider, so we do it whether it feels right or not. We're taught that to want money and material things is to be greedy so we subconsciously sabotage our own success. Or we feel confused when our material wealth doesn't make us happy.

Personal values are not a one-size-fits-all Snuggie but we hold onto them like that. Instead of revising and reworking our values to accommodate our changing lives, we cling to them like we do worn-out clothes.

I've got a maroon blazer in my closet that's been there for twenty years. Not kidding. It's the boxy kind with the shoulder pads that actually have dust on them now. It's outdated and doesn't fit but it's there anyhow, taking up space.

We do this with our values too. We build our lives around these old ideas without really examining if they still fit or make sense to the lives we want to lead now.

MOVING CLOSE TO WHAT MATTERS

When you're willing to discover and live from your deepest values, life not only becomes a more fulfilling and passionate adventure, but it also becomes easier. Decisions are clearer when you know what's fundamentally important to you. You spend less time second-guessing yourself and more time creating a life that supports the things that drive it. You live with personal integrity.

Here's the flip side: If you don't know what matters to you, you're bound to spend more time filling up on things—alcohol, drugs, shopping sprees, reality television, painful relationships, food—that you don't really want. These things provide quick bursts of happiness or relief, but always leave you feeling a bit hungry, a bit empty. It's kind of like spiritual junk food: it tastes good going in, but it isn't enough to sustain you.

That emptiness grows out of the gap between what you value and how you are actually spending your time. The wider the gap, the more difficult life becomes. This leaves a residue that makes everything feel dull or disconnected. You feel spacey, adrift, forgetful. Life is bland and boring. Uninspired. You might catch yourself behaving more defensively or blaming others. You feel unhappy, but you can't really figure out why. Resentment sets up shop. You become sick more often, and tired. When you don't know what you value, your deepest desires go unmet. That's the highway to heartbreak.

You don't have to stay that course. Start living deliberately instead of by default. Rediscover the values at work in your life.

IN THE MOMENT PRACTICE: REDISCOVERING YOUR VALUES

This is a quickie but give it five minutes of your focus, because the self-knowledge you'll gain from this exercise is powerful.

1. Think about one thing you do that brings you immense satisfaction, pleasure, happiness.
2. What is it? Is anyone with you? Where are you when you're doing it?
3. Name three things you like about this activity or moment.
4. Why is it fulfilling? What desires does it meet? For example, I like to write articles. The process fulfills my desire for knowledge, and allows me to be self-employed, which meets my desire for independence.
5. Now come up with three other ways you can fulfill those desires. In my case, reading, meditation, and traveling would also fulfill my desire for learning and independence.
6. Today, do one of these things and pay attention to how good you feel during and after.

By discovering your desires, you are also defining what you value. If you desire more time with your kids, you value family and maybe a sense of fun and play. It's likely you'll feel happier and more productive when you do things that move you closer to this value.

Here's how it works: You've always loved the sense of teamwork and creativity that came from your corporate job and the regular paycheck was nice too. You felt as though you were contributing something to the world when you were at the office, but since your son was born, work feels downright hard. You fight through the bad feelings. You're not a quitter and you know you should be grateful for the job. But you are unhappy.

Truth is, your values have shifted and you just haven't figured that out yet. If pressed, you'd say you would rather be at home with your child than at the office. Your value of family has become more important than your career. What you desire is different nowadays, so the paycheck and the other perks of the job no longer mean as much.

When you find a way to fulfill your desire for more family time, life will flow again. This might require some creative and flexible thinking, but it's doable.

PERENNIAL PRACTICE:
VALUES ASSESSMENT

Spend at least a half hour on this exercise. Understanding your values and desires will create the infrastructure for your life. Then come back to this exercise each year to understand where you are and what you need to consciously create a life that is authentic. Be willing to shift and explore and change some of these values when new insights and understandings emerge. Connect with the desires that fuel those values each day.

Start by answering this question: What matters to me now?

List them out. There are no wrong answers. Don't judge yourself. Just answer the question, on paper. Honestly. It's about getting clear and really seeing the life you're creating as compared to the life you want to create. Value money? Write it down. Value fun more than work? Make a note. This is about awareness.

Rank the things you wrote.

Put a number one by the thing you value most today. Recognize that while your core values are likely to remain the same, their ranking may change from time to time. If you place your health (a core value for many) fifth on the list, for example, and then discover you have plaque in your arteries, your health value may shoot to numero uno real quick. Work and contribution may be your number one value before you have kids; once the bambinos come along, that may all change. Be open to the changing desires in your life.

Now grade yourself.

Give yourself an A if you are consistently taking daily actions in support of those top five values. For example, if you list your health and fitness as a number one value, and you work out, eat well, get full servings of fruit and vegetables, plus a good night's sleep, each day, you're living in alignment with that value. If you list family in the top spot, but you rarely see your kids because of long hours at the office, you're not making the A grade there. Be ruthless and honest. Where are you soaring? Where are you falling short?

Look at the grades you gave yourself.

For those B's, C's, or No Passes (sounds so much better than an F), take a close look at your value and consider the things you want in your life. Perhaps the value is outdated and no longer consistent with who you are and needs replacing.

If you determine, though, that the value is solid, look then at the ways you've separated from it and figure out a few things you can do to get back on track.

Create action items. Next, list a couple of the things you will do today to live in alignment with your top values. For example, if you value spiritual growth, perhaps you'll start meditating ten minutes a day. Is physical health among the top five? Go for a walk.

Keep it up. Each day, make sure there are items on your to-do list that are consistent with your values.

TAKE DAILY ACTION

Values-based activities must become an integral part of our regular routines—habits developed by focused attention—otherwise it's too easy to get caught up in toilet cleaning or dinner making and the other things that leave you feeling wiped out instead of revitalized. Each day needs to contain pieces, or big chunks, of the things that make us feel whole. When you're aware of what those things are, even the regular chores become more meaningful. In this way, even exercise or grocery shopping or a meeting can fulfill your desires and keep you close to your values.

"When the things we do align with our values, we feel revitalized and more confident," says psychotherapist Julie Rudiger. That helps us step into our authenticity.

Part of your practice then, is to figure out which pieces fit and feel good together. Part of your exploration is to discover what you want.

WHY IT'S GOOD TO WANT

I desire more financial abundance. I desire to live with a greater sense of peace and patience. I want to contribute to the world in a bigger way. I want to keep learning. I want to grow as a woman and wife and mom. I want to feel fit and to drop another fifteen pounds. A new stove wouldn't be so bad either. Oh, and I want the kitchen cleaned, and I'd really like the cat to stop peeing in the corner of the garage.

I've got a long list of desires. Does this make me selfish? Ungrateful? Materialistic?

I don't think so. Desires so often get a bad rap. To want anything other than world peace (which would also be nice) is to be unspiritual. I don't see it that way. To desire unleashes the boundless possibilities of the Universe. When you desire something, you're reminded of what matters to you, what you value, then you can steer your life toward that. When those desires are fulfilled, you're living from a place of personal integrity and that feels good.

UNDERSTANDING THE WHY BEHIND THE WANT

It's usually easy to identify what a person values by watching what they do to get what they want. If they value family, they may organize family dinners and find time to play with the kids. If they value security or status, they may choose well-paying jobs, fancy cars, or a big house.

What is harder to know is why people care about what they care about in the first place. This is much more personal. What is behind his drive for money? Why did she drop a career to be a stay-at-home mom? Why is he training for that marathon?

Money, for example, can support the value of security, freedom, or contribution. I know plenty of people who are motivated to earn more, not so that they can buy fancy stuff, but so that they can do more for their family members and the charities they support.

I was compelled to return to work for a few hours a day when my daughter was young—not because I valued my career more than my family, but because I valued both. I discovered that when my desires for creation and contribution weren't met through my work, I didn't feel so good and that kept me from being the best mother I could be. When I lived more in alignment with each of my values, I was happier and more successful in every area of my life, including motherhood.

In other words, it's none of your beeswax what someone else values and why. Your main mission is to figure it out for yourself.

IN THE MOMENT PRACTICE: DIG UP YOUR DESIRES

Ask yourself these questions: What do you want? Why do you want it? What value does this support? Write in your journal about your answers.

IMPERFECTIONS LEAD TO INSIGHT

But do take notice if the things you're spending the bulk of your time on now no longer feel good, or are incongruent with who you are. Pay attention to that. The less-than-perfect things in your life can serve as a compass, pointing you toward what you need to do now to live a life consistent with your values. Sometimes we must make an external shift to keep up with our internal changes.

THE RULES OF DESIRE

Our desires can help us stay this course. They make it obvious what we value. Still many of us are a little shy about wanting too much or even declaring our desires aloud. Sometimes we even apologize for having too much, or becoming too successful. We're afraid of being judged as shallow or materialistic or frivolous or ungrateful or greedy.

Imagine, though, the momentum we would all experience if the Earth was filled with people who were all pursuing their greatest desires, dreams, and passions and connecting wholly to their values-based happiness. Your dreams would inspire my dreams. Your actions would support mine. Life on this planet would be all kinds of awesome.

So before you beat yourself up over declaring what you want, consider how your values contribute to everyone else and keep in mind the Rules of Desire:

1. Desiring more doesn't prevent you from feeling immense gratitude, joy, and appreciation for what you already have.
2. Contrast can illuminate our desires and values. We get sick, so we desire health. We feel lonely, so we desire intimacy. Contrast shows us what we truly want.
3. My desires do not derail your desires.
4. There is enough for each of us, at any time, to have all that we want. The Universe is unlimited, and because we are connected to Source, we too are ever expanding, unlimited energy from spirit. There is enough for everyone, even if we all want the same stuff.
5. Desire fuels creativity, inspiration, curiosity, gratitude, and awareness. When you want, you get excited. You start finding solutions and connecting with others. You

become inspired and inspiring. The expansive nature of desire and the pursuit of our desires is world-changing.

6. Reflective desire connects us to our deepest values and loads of good feelings. We feel good when we live in alignment with our values by fulfilling our desires. Out of that comes a cyclical process of loving and thanking and inspiring and appreciating. Desiring then becomes a passing around of positive energy.

7. Knowing the "why" behind your desire enhances the feeling behind it. Often it's not only the big money we want in a job, but the joy that comes from doing work that is meaningful. Our desires for emotional well-being and spiritual enlightenment work the same way. My desire to learn and practice compassion satisfies my value of spiritual growth and connection.

8. Go big. Get in touch with your deepest values and desires and go for it. As Rabbi Brad Hirschfield says, "If you expect to see the outcomes of all of your dreams and wishes, then you are dreaming too small."

When we dream big from our value system, and respond with awe and gratitude and appreciation for all that shows up, life not only becomes more fun, but it also becomes steeped in meaning.

IN THE MOMENT PRACTICE:
DECLARING WHAT MATTERS

Now you've done the work, pondered your desires, and evaluated how and when you're living close to your values and when you're out of alignment. Next, take ten minutes and write down the values you hold close.

Then each day, take a look at this list. Contemplate each item and consider how that value is appearing in your life during the day. See how it shows up in your actions. Move back toward it when you catch yourself turning away. This way, your values and desires become a conscious part of your personal operating system.

ONE PATH:
FROM DEVASTATION TO DREAM JOB

In less than a minute, Jessica Riesenbeck's entire life shifted. When the owners of the small prosthetic/orthotic business where she worked as an office manager announced that they had sold their shop to a large corporation eight years ago, Jessica's salary was cut, her vacation time reduced, and the medical benefits that she and her husband were depending on to ease the costs of the birth of her second child were wiped out. She was panicked, angry, and scrambling to provide for her family.

In the midst of the fear and betrayal she felt, Jessica also got clear: Her family was her number one priority and she would never again jeopardize their security. Motivated by that insight and inspired by an article she read in *TIME* Magazine, the Houston, Ohio, woman decided to quit her job and build her own business as a virtual assistant.

At first she struggled to make money, to stay afloat in the fear, and gain the confidence she needed to run her own shop. But as her business slowly developed, so did her vision. If Jessica was going to be successful in business, she realized it needed to be built around *her* desires, *her* values.

"When I remembered who I was, I realized that my values are me and my business is a representation of that. I decided I was going to communicate that in how I worked with my friends and clients. I tell them that my family comes first. I'm up-front about my priorities. It's cost me some business, but it's brought me far more. The clients I work with now share those values and respect and care about me as a person."

One of those clients is the life coach Martha Beck, who was referred to Jessica. After working with Beck and some other coaches, Jessica studied and became a certified life coach herself. She is now teaching other moms to draw from their core values, talents, and desires to run their own virtual assistants' businesses.

Jessica works from home, sets her own hours, and loves going to work in the morning. She sometimes thinks about that "boring, comfortable" job she says she "settled for" years ago. She thinks about the fear and anger she felt during the shake-up. She knows, too, it happened just the way it needed to.

"Everything happens for a reason," she says. "You might not know what it is for a while, but my reason, the reason I had to go through all this, was so I could start living my life. Really living it. I knew the possibility was out there, that I could like my job and keep my values to spend time with my family. It wasn't easy, but I've done it. Now I know I can take on anything."

Chapter 11:

Finding Meaning in Mistakes

There is not one big cosmic meaning for all, there
is only the meaning we each give to our life, an
individual meaning, an individual plot, like an individual novel, a book for each person.

—ANAIS NIN

By now you've probably figured out that life is not like an
easy-to-follow dot-to-dot. You don't move from number
one to number two. It doesn't form a clear picture that
you can color in with rainbow stripes. It gets a little catawam-
pus and crooked. You misread the numbers, make mistakes,
and fail to draw a straight line.

In the end it all looks like the picture my five-year-old puts together. Start at number 1, hit 2 and 3, draw a rigid line across to number 43 ("because I wanted to go by the flowers"), then realize you must circle back around to 35, 34, maybe hit 12 along the way. Ultimately, all the numbers get covered and the picture does take shape. It's just not the one you expected to see. Still, it's your picture just the same. The one you created, the one you get to play with. And, what you see in it, how you think about it—whether you focus on its beauty and originality, or how you got it wrong—will determine the meaning the picture has. You can see life like this too. Your life can be a work of art, a contribution, and a worthwhile experience, or a failed experiment. It all depends on the meaning you ascribe.

MEANING "OF" LIFE VERSUS MEANING "IN" LIFE

I can't begin to tell you about the meaning *of* life, because I don't have a clue as to why a Universe that includes rain forests and stars and dolphins, as well as pizza and reality television, was created in the first place. I'm happy about it and I like it, the funkiness of it all, especially the stars-pizza part, but I'm more interested in finding meaning in the moments of the life I'm already living. I'm curious about what powers people up, helps them create fulfilling lives, and helps them thrive despite adversity and trouble and bad days and irritating people in the checkout line.

Meaning *in* life is dependent on how we see and interpret the world. But what creates meaning or leads to a meaningful life is vast and varied. What matters to me, after all, is different than what matters to you. This is one reason there is no single definition or standard strategy among philosophers and psychologists as to what meaning in life really is and how to capture it. Though we all have the same basic needs of love and nourishment and shelter and safety, it is the specific ways those things play out in our lives that influences the meaning they hold for each of us. Meaning, therefore, is personal and organic.

For example, a hamburger to a hungry boy is going to come laced with a different meaning than it will for a boy who eats hamburgers every night for dinner. The meaning we place on the experiences in our lives determines the lives we're going to live.

To live a life without meaning is to live a life that feels empty and barren. On the other hand, people who do have meaning in their lives, or are actively engaged in the search for meaning, tend to be more satisfied, says Michael Steger, a Colorado State University associate professor who studies aspects of meaning in life. They tend to feel better and experience greater well-being and less mental decline. Even their risk for Alzheimer's disease drops.

> **POWER UP:**
>
> Meaning in life comes from how you interpret an experience or happening. Our feelings, attitudes, beliefs, and actions often emerge from the meanings we assign to these events.

ASKING THE BIG QUESTIONS

Meaning helps us to find ourselves and then to be comfortable with what we find. Meaning prompts us to live a life that is close to our values and talents and passions and desires. Those things move us toward our purpose. And in all that, meaning helps us face and endure the tough times in life. This is where the practice of imperfection comes into play because even the imperfect and despair-filled moments can have profound meaning. Challenges have value. Nothing is wasted or worthless. With meaning, we can transcend the darkest days.

But, like so many other aspects of personal development and spiritual growth, discovering the meaning in your life is not a passive endeavor. It requires contemplation (you can do this with a glass of wine or while doing the dishes), introspection, and awareness.

The search for meaning is about looking at what is and discovering the wisdom in the moment, if any exists. That takes open-mindedness and curiosity and it starts by asking the Big Questions:

What matters to you?

How do you feel about it?

What will you focus on?

What will you do?

When we determine what matters most to us, and there can be lots of things—health, relationships, contribution, are usually the biggies—then we tend to focus on those things. We define them, see where they are in our lives, and throw our emotional, spiritual, and physical energy behind them. We are motivated to take action, to get away from what feels icky and move toward the things that resonate. This is where the good stuff happens.

HOW MEANING MOVES US

We get fired up about the things that create meaning in our lives. We protect them, love them, and engage with them. They move us. We may not realize just how much, until we are on the verge of losing what we value most. Sometimes we don't think about the perks of our job until layoffs loom, or we fail to see all that she does for us until she says she's walking out the door.

In this way, meaning and our search for it becomes a

motivating factor. When we care, we call a counselor to help us through the tough spot because our marriage means a shot at love and intimacy and social connection. We eat more salads without dressing because a healthy body means we'll live longer and have more to give.

Meaning, too, helps us make sense of our experience. It allows for a different interpretation. Without it my cancer scare would have just stressed me out, but because of the meaning I tattooed onto my experience it became something valuable and life changing. I became aware of how much fun I'm having here with the people and things in my life. I began to appreciate my body differently. I encouraged others. I stopped putting things off. Well, most things. The experience didn't inspire me to clean the hall closet, but it did cause me to think about how I want my daughter to feel when she's with me. It started me working on this book. The meaning in the melanoma then was one of opportunity.

By unraveling the moments of our lives like this, Steger says meaning can foster satisfaction and fulfillment. It's expansive and makes room for spirituality. It helps us to connect to something larger than self. Though a meaningful life does not necessarily ensure a happy one.

> ## POWER UP:
>
> Meaning makes your darkest moments easier to bear. When you believe that something can come from the hardship, you seek the blessing or the wisdom in the experience. By doing this, you are no longer sitting in the muck, you are moving through it.

PAIN CAN BE PART OF IT

I'm not saying this kind of introspection or awareness is easy. Often the things we find meaning in leave stretch marks of uncertainty and growth. Divorce, job loss, pain, struggle, and sickness are rotten ways to experience meaning. But, if the bad stuff is bound to happen, it's reassuring to know that something powerful and positive can come from it.

My melanoma led me to encourage others to get screened. Candy Lightner lost her teenage daughter to a drunk driver in 1980. Her despair propelled her to form Mothers Against Drunk Driving. Ann Quasman used the story of her sexual assault to help other women, and a friend of mine found her passion as a nutrition coach by exploring treatment options to help her son.

When the ick hits, we try to make sense of it. That search can keep us from falling into an abyss. It doesn't necessarily make the pain go away, but it does ease suffering.

SEEKING THE MEANINGFUL MOMENTS

Living a life filled with these kinds of meaningful moments though isn't some arbitrary experience. You get to choose which moments matter. You get to determine what the meaning is. This is an empowering place to be. It is the very opposite of disconnect. It's engagement. It's choosing the life you want to lead.

Here's how it works: Your husband makes the coffee for you each morning, though he's never had a cup of it in his life. You can decide to blow this off, and take it for granted. You can decide that he's wasting his time when he could be doing a more important chore like unloading the dishwasher. Or, you could recognize that his coffee making is a gesture of love. He knows you love coffee. He makes it for you instead of doing something for himself. The simple little cup of coffee then means that he loves you.

Now which answer feels the best? You can, of course, see less than. The coffee can be a time waster. The guy who cuts you off on the freeway can be a sign that the whole world is out to get you. The job loss can mean you're incapable. You are free to pick. Be wise then, with your choices. If you feel like your life is unfulfilled, if you're despairing and doubting your purpose, go back and check out your beliefs and then see the meaning you've assigned to these moments of your life.

If you simply see your flaws and mistakes as failures, with no hope of improvement, then that is a bummer. What if those same failures provided opportunities for growth and humor and knowledge? What if they offered the insight you need to change the world? Doesn't that just feel a little more hopeful?

IN THE MOMENT PRACTICE: FINDING MEANING IN THE MUNDANE

Pull out a pen and paper, and quickly write down your top three values or priorities. Now, for each one, write down two things that you've got to get done today in support of that priority.

For example: One of my values is my family. And today, I will do the grocery shopping, and wash the outfit my daughter wants to wear tomorrow. My physical health is another priority, so I'll exercise for a half hour, and eat a healthy lunch.

Now look at the so-called mundane chores you put on the list. For me, laundry is definitely one. But each one of these tasks also supports my top priorities, the things I value most.

When laundry becomes a way of loving my daughter, the chore feels more meaningful than mundane. Instead of "having to cook dinner again," you are actually nourishing your family. Instead of "I should work out," you can see the exercise as an opportunity to continue living well.

HOW TO FIND MEANING

Only you can determine what is meaningful in your life, but I've found meaning becomes clearer when you're open and honest and living authentically. When I'm operating from my values, engaged in my passions, and paying attention, I'm a more flexible, creative thinker and meaning often materializes.

Here's how it works: Your mammogram shows breast cancer. You're scared and totally ticked off at the gods. Treatment is difficult. You share your story and those honest feelings with a friend. She's reminded to get her own exam. During it, doctors discover a tiny lump. She has a lumpectomy and complete recovery. Because you were authentic in your time of trouble, your experience created something bigger than the cancer. Your experience became about life, rather than illness.

You might not see it right away. This stuff doesn't just appear in thought bubbles over your head or phantom messages written in the clouds. You have to go looking for the meaning behind the madness; however, this search is exciting. It starts from a knowing that things are always bigger than they appear and it's a road paved by faith.

Here are some other tools to guide you in your search for meaning:

Become Mindful. Create pauses throughout your day to be present in the moment. Quiet allows for contemplation and reflection and helps us move closer to the meaning in our lives.

Become Curious. Look for connections and synchronicities. Interpret experiences. Ask questions. See the new within the familiar. Seek the why behind the happening and you'll see threads of meaning wrapped around life's most mundane moments. Be playful with this. Don't start overanalyzing, like the English professor who looks for nuance in every sentence ever written by Virginia Woolf. Just notice what you don't know and start the study.

Remain Open-Minded and Accepting. Live with awareness. Be open to all of life, even when it's uncomfortable, unhappy, and imperfect. Uncomfortable moments can motivate us to take action that can result in meaningful experiences.

Let It Be. If you interpret everything as a sign of something deeper, you're going to become a little unstable and weird. Not everything holds deeper meaning. If you spill the milk, it doesn't mean you should stop drinking the stuff. Usually, a wrong number is a wrong number, not a message from the cosmos. A fight with your partner doesn't have to be an omen of troubles to come. Just let it be.

WHAT TO TAKE FROM ALL OF THIS

Just about everyone I've ever interviewed during my twenty-year career as a journalist, from giant pumpkin growers to professional poker players, medical experts to embezzlers, as well as arborists, roller derby women, mothers and musicians (I know, a varied lot), has recounted at least one ultra-profound meaningful experience which they say changed their lives.

Usually these were little things—one read an article in a magazine that led to a new hobby, another asked a friend a question and got a surprising answer, another was dealing with a child's tantrums, and another was looking for relief after heartbreak. But these little moments yielded great meaning to these people. That meaning prompted them to make a move, to search for more, to define their desires and values, and to take action that shaped their lives and helped them survive struggles. Not all were happy. The embezzler was not a big fan of prison, but she says getting caught for her crime helped her kick her gambling addiction and heal her life. Meaning abounds.

Go looking for it in your life. When you can merge your life experience with meaning by asking: "How does this serve me?" "What can I take from this?" "What can I give back as a result of this?" "Who will I be because of this?" even the toughest, ickiest, messiest, imperfect events and happenings become worthwhile.

PERENNIAL PRACTICE:
THE WEB OF GRATITUDE

Take out your journal and a pen and set aside twenty minutes for this exercise in thankfulness.

Gratitude is the surest way to heal your heart and soul and to move your focus to what is good and working in your life. It's also the fastest way, I've found, to make a difference in your day. When we commit to a regular gratitude practice, we start to see the webs of meaning sticking to all the crannies in our lives and we find even more reasons to be grateful for all that we have.

For example, when I lost four magazine assignments, and all of my income, in a twenty-four-hour period, I got nervous, then I freaked. Then, after a few deep breaths, I got curious and started asking The Big Questions: What is the meaning behind this? What can I do with this? What is working?

The answers to those questions helped me to get clear about my situation and helped me to recognize all that I did have to be grateful for (a husband with a job, a little money in the bank, breath in my lungs, and mint chocolate chip in the freezer).

From that place of gratitude, I could start seeing the possibilities the lost work provided. It freed up my schedule to follow a dream I'd had for decades—the writing of this book. When I gave thanks for my life as it was, I could see the meaning behind the lost assignments, and a dismal situation became a life-changing experience.

Now, you try it. In this exercise you'll have a chance to begin a practice of gratitude and find those gifts of meaning in your own life.

1. List ten things you are thankful for.
2. How many of those things evolved out of less than perfect circumstances?
3. Pick one to write about. Describe how it came to be in your life.
4. What did you learn from it?
5. What did you do as a result of it?
6. What meaning does it hold for you?

ONE PATH:
FROM DARKNESS TO LIGHT

When Rhonda Sciortino was six months old, her mother left her at a neighbor's house and never returned. She was taken in by her grandfather, a mentally ill, depressed man who parented through abuse and neglect, and her grandmother, an alcoholic, who ultimately drank herself to death.

Life was filled with hunger, struggle, and pain. "I lived in a very dark place," Rhonda says. "Literally the house was dark, there were often no lights because the electric bill hadn't been paid. It was a filthy, oppressive place."

When she was about six years old, Rhonda was temporarily placed with a foster family who introduced her to the lighter side of life. "They lived in a clean house. There was plenty of food, they didn't fight with each other—I remember watching them interact with one another as though they really enjoyed being together," Rhonda, fifty, says.

One day the man in the foster home encouraged her to search for the meaning in her own life. "Young lady," he said, "you better quit feeling sorry for yourself. You were put here for a reason, and you better be about finding out what it is."

The family also took her to a Christian church, where Rhonda says, "meeting Jesus was a turning point."

Although she was ultimately placed back into the

abusive home environment, Rhonda never forgot those people, their influence, or the role of Jesus Christ in her life.

She believed that there was something more for her, something better. She discovered just what that was when, as an insurance professional, she received a thank you note from the CEO of a children's home. She had helped the facility keep operating by saving it thousands of dollars in insurance premiums.

For Rhonda, that thank you note was infused with meaning. She quit her job, and started her own insurance agency, founded solely to help the people and organizations that help children. Today, she continues that work in her "dream job" as The National Child Welfare Specialist for Markel Insurance Company.

She lives with her husband of more than twenty years in a light-filled home overlooking California's Pacific Coast and she is a loving mother and grandmother. Rhonda is no longer haunted by her darkness-filled childhood, and no longer angry.

"I've forgiven them for the abuse and neglect," Rhonda says. "I value all my life experiences, including the bad, because I gained an understanding and empathy that could not be acquired any other way."

The resourcefulness, self-reliance, and persistence that she developed to survive her childhood have also helped her succeed in business and with her life's purpose.

It's her unwavering belief in God, Rhonda says, that drives her to help and inspire others through her books, speeches, training programs, and affiliations.

She is the founder of The Successful Survivors Foundation and supports Foster Care Alumni of America, Teen Leadership Foundation, Birth Choice, The National Foster Parent Association, and other organizations.

"My life is better now," Rhonda says, "than I ever dreamed possible."

Chapter 12:

Living with Spirit

Don't judge each day by the harvest you reap but
by the seeds that you plant.

—ROBERT LOUIS STEVENSON

It's 8 o'clock and my husband is getting our daughter ready
for bed with books and songs and tales of pirates and Super Boo Boo, the magical cat. I head to the bedroom, to
meditate. The gurus and spiritual experts refer to meditation
as a practice. And the practice comes with perks. Peace, health,
wisdom, well-being, and a few little things like that.

Thing is, I no longer get a lot of practice time. Like so
many others, my days are filled with work and breakfast mak-

ing and bill paying and cat-litter changing. I try to spend a few minutes each day to connect with my husband—usually while we're folding clothes or sitting in front of the television—and a few more for myself, sometimes in meditation, sometimes watching, truth be told, a drama on television.

Meditation is much tougher than watching T.V. To meditate I have to find a quiet space, Challenge No. 1, and wade through my own crazy thoughts, Challenge No. 2, while remembering to breathe.

Sit still. Quiet now. Breathe. Follow the breath. Ommm. Silence. Blank mind, follow the thoughts. Not *those* thoughts. Quiet now. Did I turn off the oven? Not now. Breathe. Ahh. Did I ruin Sweet P's life by ordering her to eat the salmon? Stop. Quiet now. Breathe. Ahh, my mind is blank, empty. Is this meditation? Am I doing this right?

After a few minutes of this kind of mental banter I hear, "Mawwwmy," followed by tiny hands pounding on my door. Meditation is officially over.

This is how it goes for me some nights—okay, many nights—unless I wait until the dishes are done, and my daughter is in bed, for good. On those late nights, when I escape to meditate, I do manage to quiet my thoughts, by falling asleep. And, there are those times too when my practice is peaceful and even revealing.

My meditation practice, at best, reflects my own spiritual

growth and development—unpredictable, inconsistent, imperfect. But each time I sit down to practice I'm becoming aware of my spirit.

WHAT IS SPIRITUALITY?

Spirituality is about living with this awareness in deep relationship with yourself—the self that is both created by and connected to the Universal Source of all that is. From this place you recognize that everything is interconnected. We are all one. You are part of source energy, just as all of that is a part of you.

When you touch your spirit from this place of knowing, you are then guided by this higher energy, instead of Ego. This energy is fueled by love and compassion, gratitude and expansion. It is not about gossip, or image, or control. It isn't about being right or better than.

"It's not conceptual, it's not intellectual, it's a state of knowing with a capital K," says Paul Hertel, an interfaith minister and spiritual healer, who also happens to be the research editor at a New York-based magazine. "There is a certainty in my being, an inner sense of Knowing, peace. Everybody has a different experience of that Knowing, but anybody can open themselves up to it. Spirituality is staying in the presence of the Divine, or keeping that connection to God or spirit as often and as long as you can."

You don't have to do anything to become spiritual; it's part of our makeup, just like brown eyes and curly hair. But, if you want to live a spiritual life and experience the interconnectedness that comes with that higher energy, practice is essential. People who live a spiritually based life use practices that help focus their attention and awareness to keep them close to this Source energy.

This requires commitment, because some days you're bound to wake up bloated and tired and ticked at the world. Living close to spirit doesn't insulate you from bad feelings or pain or insecurity. It doesn't instantly transform the bad moments into bliss, nor does it keep us from getting into trouble for our own poor choices. It does, however, keep us from making more of them. And it offers solutions and ways of coping with the trouble spots. Instead of erupting in anger, you may choose to be compassionate. Instead of reacting with intolerance, you may find a way to love. When the world seems a mess of mismatched socks and stressful moments, a spiritual connection offers solace.

> ## POWER UP:
> Spirituality is a practical approach to living that can be accessed and strengthened through deliberate attention and the focus that comes from a daily practice.

In this way, spirituality is a practical way to live. Plenty of studies indicate that people with a strong faith or religious belief fare better health-wise and report greater well-being and happiness than those who don't have a spiritual connection. A Gallup Poll showed people in Europe and North America who were "religiously active" were twice as likely to describe themselves as "very happy" than those with no religious ties. University of Toronto psychologists found that "believing in God can help block anxiety and minimize stress." According to their report and another study, patients with clinical depression showed that a belief in God improved response to medical treatment. Numerous studies also show that people with strong religious beliefs have smoother recovery times after surgery.

But you don't need religion to tap into the sacredness of every day. Our ability to cultivate compassion and gratitude, to live from love, and to experience joy and wonder and awe—in any moment—is perhaps the most powerful aspect of spirituality. Those things root us in the present and connect us to our God and each other. Those things are available to each of us.

LIVING DELIBERATELY OR BY DEFAULT

So this is where the rubber meets the road, or the olive hits the gin, because it's not enough to read this book, or others. It's not enough to attend seminars and listen to podcasts. It's not enough to study spirituality; you've got to live it.

"Spirituality is not meant to be separate," Hertel says. "Day-to-day spirituality helps me to be more loving and able to be more authentic and open. The expression of my spirituality is always my focus."

Daily practice can keep you closer to your own spirituality and give you something to draw from when things feel difficult.

GUIDELINES TO GET YOU STARTED

Before you put your practice into play, though, know this: the only way to screw up this spiritual stuff is to limit your awareness and close yourself off. Otherwise, just get out of your own way and open to the essence of all that you are.

Drop the desire for perfection. Sometimes meditation is going to reveal nothing more than how scatterbrained you are, if you can even sit through it at all. Chances are you will at some point lash out in anger, even when you are committed to compassion. The spiritual path is not always easy or clear. That's why you *practice,* silly.

A spiritual practice is how we develop the spiritual habits that become the guiding behaviors in our lives. This takes time, which means you won't always get it right, immediately. That's okay, give yourself a break and just get started.

Release outcomes. Practices don't always yield obvious results. But it's the doing that matters most of all. Detach from outcomes. Burrow into this practice. Be present to the experience and pay attention to what you're doing rather than what you might get out of it.

Don't judge. A meditation doesn't have to be easy or hard, it is simply a meditation. Prayers are not right or wrong; they are prayers. A spiritual practice is composed of situations to be experienced. Just let it be. Don't judge or compare your practice to some medicine man in Bali or the meditating mama in your playgroup. Just do what you do and be with it.

Be consistently persistent. Keep going. You don't train for a marathon in a day. You won't pick up the nuances of a new language in a twenty-minute session. Learning is a process. It's about putting in the practice until it starts working in our lives automatically. To help establish the habit, make time for spiritual development every day and find a place—this can be a hallway, the shower, the car, a designated meditation room, or an altar—for quiet practice. The practices below are designed to work for you even in the midst of a busy day, and once you build them in, you'll discover how this practice will support you in everything you do.

Right now, I'm using shorter practices scattered throughout my day, usually before a meal or at other transition times. This helps me stay aware, it keeps me connected to spirit all day, and it eases my stress when things are a bit out of balance or full-on whacked out. I know others who do an hour meditation when they first get out of bed in the morning. A friend uses her commute as a time of prayer and contemplation. Find the time.

MORNING RITUALS

Brent Mather starts each morning with a thirty-minute meditation. I start mine by hitting the snooze button. Good enough. Everybody does it their own way. But it's important to have a way. And once you're lucid enough, I believe it's big-time powerful to create some morning rituals to connect to the Universe and get clear about how you want to experience the moments of your life.

When I do finally get my eyes open, I lay in the quiet of my bed and give thanks. Gratitude is a powerful pick-me-up and I use it throughout the day to remind me what's working and to connect me to the goodness.

Three Keys to Gratitude: Be specific. Name your items slowly and deliberately out loud or in your mind's eye. Feel what they mean to you.

After I give thanks, I visualize the experience I want to have during the day and a couple of the things I want to accomplish. I know unexpected things are going to come into my life and instead of visualizing every move or outcome I create more of a sense of how I want to feel during all of it. I think about things like compassion and patience and love. I think about how I want to approach life with an openness and curiosity, instead of stress and frustration. This is similar to setting an intention. It reminds me of what I want to pay attention to, what I want to accomplish, and what I will do to live from my values and spirit while moving through the world. It's like sending a flare out to the Universe, and once it's afire you're free to create that in your life both consciously and unconsciously.

While I often set intentions before phone calls or meetings or writing sessions, my morning intentions are usually the big picture kind of deal and I keep it very simple:

I intend to live with compassion and patience.

I intend to be kind to myself, and others.

I intend to nourish my body with healthy activity and food.

Once I'm clear about how I want to move through the day, I release my intention and move into the action.

My morning ritual also includes some light stretching, which could be anything from putting on my socks, to shoulder rolls and twists. I drink a bottle of water and make my way to breakfast. All of this takes less than ten minutes but I've been known to do it in two when I'm running late. By taking a moment to center myself in this world, by making a conscious connection to my spirit, the morning rituals have become a peaceful and powerful way to start my day.

COFFEE BREAKS AND SPIRITUAL QUICKIES

There are plenty of other short practices to use during your morning break or anytime when you have a few minutes.

Prayer. Hertel sometimes says a short prayer in the hallway at work. I have prayed while sipping from a mug of coffee and listening to the birds on my deck *and* in the closet while pulling on my sweats. Prayer can be a long period of conversation or contemplation, sometimes I do this before bed, or it can occur in a moment.

POWER UP:

Prayer is a communication with the divine. It's a pause, where you acknowledge and connect to the higher power, whatever that looks like to you.

"Anything can be a prayer," says Rabbi Brad Hirschfield. And while religious traditions have specific rituals associated with them, prayer doesn't have to follow strict rules to be powerful. It can be as simple as a pause, a grace before a meal, an awareness of the spirit within, and a moment to acknowledge and connect to the divine.

But, "if it leaves you feeling more dead than alive, more angry than loving, you are probably not praying well. If it leaves you feeling renewed or even discomforted, it's okay," Hirschfield says. "Prayer is not spiritual Percocet. Sometimes it is. Sometimes it works that way, but that's not all it is. It doesn't always leave you feeling better, but it always leaves you feeling more."

Prayer is an ideal way to connect with spirit during the in-between times. Don't just pray when you're feeling lost and confused, keep the dialogue going all day long. If you are in a bad space, articulating those feelings in a prayer can often provide an emotional release that makes way for clarity and calm.

Belly Breathing. Sometimes called diaphragmatic breathing or abdominal breathing, this is a quick way to ease your stress response and develop spiritual awareness. Take a break for a minute or ten, sit with your shoulders back, and breathe deeply concentrating on expanding your belly. Pull air slowly in through your nose, exhaling out of your mouth. This not only feels good, but physiologically it also brings more oxygen to your brain, which eases the stress response.

LUNCH WITH A SIDE OF MINDFULNESS

Use your midafternoon break on a quiet combo of belly breathing and mindfulness.

Mindfulness. Be still and become present to what is. Use your senses to provide a visceral experience in the moment. Our stress, anxiety, frustration (as well as the good feelings we have) are products of our thoughts. By returning to our bodies and our environment we get out of our mind and into our spirit and the present moment.

IN THE MOMENT PRACTICE: PALMING THE PRESENT MOMENT

Mindfulness expert Donald Altman recommends this quick exercise from his book, *The Mindfulness Code*:

Take a breath as you place your palms together in front of the heart center. Notice the warmth between the palms.

Press harder noticing how the tension goes up the wrists and into the arms and shoulders.

Then slowly release, feeling the coolness in the hands as the heat dissipates. In this moment the focus brings you into the body, and away from obsessive thinking and stress.

Three Keys to Mindfulness: Move into the present moment by paying attention to your body. Don't judge what you see or sense. Let thoughts come in and out without attachment.

Move into Nature. My lunchtime break usually includes getting up and out of the chair and moving outside, even if it's just to stand on the porch, watching a slug slime across the path. I'm not a fan of spiders or crawly things and I don't like cold or mud, but no matter, moving the body a bit, breathing in the fresh air, and taking a moment to notice the tips of the trees blowing in the breeze or the bee on the chrysanthemum can remind you of the universal connection we all have. Knowing you are just one marvel in a Universe of many is a powerfully uplifting thing. It's a good stress reliever too.

Allow for Flexibility. Though most of my days include meditation and a gratitude practice, my schedule right now is as fluid and flexible as my daily life. I used to meditate an hour after dinner each night. Now, I spend that hour with my family and fit in a five-to-twenty minute meditation during my lunch break. Until this last year, I never had a morning ritual and my visualization exercises were done sporadically. Right now, those things are a part of my day—every day. As I learn new things and expand into my own spirituality, I leave room for the practices to shift and expand, as well. This feels good. It saves space for novelty and insight. While spirituality does grow from practice and discipline, it doesn't have to feel hard or arduous. It can feel reinvigorating like play. It's a fluid, dynamic way of being.

EVENING PRACTICE

Right now my evening practice involves working on the cross-word from the newspaper and going to bed. Not too inspiring, I know, but it's where I am right now. Before I fall asleep, I also do a gratitude exercise where I name specific things that showed up in my day. I say a short prayer, one I heard from Wayne Dyer: "Thank you, God, for all that I have and all that I am." Sometimes I do some inspirational reading or journaling.

If you're looking to add a spiritual nightcap to the end of your day, consider these two practices:

Journaling: There are lots of different approaches to journaling and most will help you foster clarity and connect to spirit. You can do this as a free-write exercise, where you keep your hand writing across the page for a set amount of time without stopping. Or you can pour out your dreams and concerns and feelings on the page until you're done. Gratitude lists, where you jot down what you're thankful for, are a good-feeling way to end the day. It's useful, too, I think, to start with a spiritual prompt to help you develop a deeper awareness of your experience. Ask yourself a question like: How did I behave compassionately today? What do I most need to know about my life and my purpose? What am I denying? How did I live close to my values today?

Pose the questions and let the answers flow. Don't judge what you write in the journal. Just notice it. When we ask the

Big Questions, our intuition often speaks to us through our words and we get Big Answers.

Meditation: I know, I know, you just don't have the time for meditation, or you are not good at sitting still, or it doesn't work for you, or you can't do it right. I've heard all the excuses. Heck, I invented a few. Still, I meditate. If a Type-A-to-the-third-degree person like me finds this helpful, it's worth trying. I'm telling you it's a life changer.

Here are some quick meditation tips:

Sit still.

Be quiet.

Sit still longer.

There. That's it. Don't make it more complicated than it is. It's a simple practice but it is not easy to do. It is difficult, because our Ego kicks in and our mind kicks up with thoughts like: Did I remember to record that show? I never should have bought those shoes. Why does alfredo sauce have to be so high in calories? With time this mindless chatter slows down and things get quieter. But some days I still feel like I have a carnival barker screaming in my head.

Meditation is an essential practice, because eventually it helps quiet this mind chatter so that we can hear our inner voices and develop greater awareness and insight.

Once you've established a practice of sitting in silence for at least five minutes a day (work up to more time as you get your meditative muscles in shape), then you can go deeper and study different techniques and styles, like transcendental, Japa, or sound and moving meditation. It's all good. But you can start your meditation practice right now, without any rules or training. Really.

PERENNIAL PRACTICE: MEDITATION TIME

Find twenty minutes (set the alarm on your cell phone or computer or maybe a real live, old-fashioned clock so that you know when your time is up and don't spend the entire session looking at your watch, yes, I know that trick too) when you won't be disturbed and give meditation a try. These guidelines can help.

Get comfortable. Sit on a chair, or lay down, if you feel like it. I like to sit on a firm but comfortable surface, with shoes off, feet on the floor, back straight so I can easily and comfortably take deep breaths and stay alert.

Close your eyes. Some do meditate with their eyes open or while looking at a picture of Buddha, or some other image. In the beginning, though, I think it works better to close your eyes and focus on the space there behind your eyelids.

Breathe deeply from your diaphragm. Early on I was so obsessed with breathing right that I usually hyperventilated. Let's just say that isn't necessary. Instead, take slow breaths. Feel your stomach moving in and out. These breaths are cleansing, rhythmic, and they also heighten your state by infusing your cells with oxygen.

Focus on something. Many people focus on their breath. Deepak Chopra talks about the "I Am" meditation where you simply repeat and focus on those words as you breathe in and out. Wayne Dyer follows the Lord's Prayer in one of his meditations and guides you to focus on the spaces—the gap—between the words of the prayer. The minute you begin meditating your thoughts will begin jerking you in all directions as though you're holding the leashes of a dozen dogs all headed different ways. Focus brings you back.

Notice your thoughts. When you catch a renegade thought coming through, and they will, roughly a billion times a session, bless it and imagine your breath blowing it gently out of your head, clearing your mind. Then return to your focus, to your breath.

Exhale. Ahh.

That is meditation. If you felt tense, a little restless, uptight, and wondering what the heck is so good about meditating, then you were successful. This is how it starts—for all of us. This is why practice is necessary. With repetition and deliberate attention, your body and brain learn to become quieter so you can hear your spirit speak.

DIFFERENCE MAKERS

On the days when you feel as though you can't find the time for a longer practice, these short practices can provide a mind/body/spirit alignment that can make a real difference in your day:

Say "thank you." Within the context of everything you do, pause—really slow down—and say thank you. Look the checker in the eye, take a breath, and say, "thank you." Pause before a meal and give thanks to the farmers and the Earth and the animals or the Coca-Cola distributor who brought the food to your table. Say "thank you."

Get quiet. This is one of the greatest, most important gifts I give myself each day. Sometimes my quiet time comes in the three minutes I have in the car en route to the school. Other times it's in the shower, or a few moments of solitude between work and lunch. It is essential. Turn off the phone, and television, be quiet. Be still if you can, for as long as you can. Even a minute of solitude in the car or while washing the dishes can be helpful, but try to find time for at least ten minutes a day. If you can't find time away, simply close your eyes for a minute, sit quietly, take some belly breaths.

Create triggers. Living a life closer to spirit is all about awareness. It's about noticing and acknowledging your thoughts, pausing to become aware of your breath and emotions, recognizing what you're grateful for and what you love.

Triggers are those symbols or signs that can move us into

instant awareness of spirit and source. Find your triggers—a special song, a repeated number, a special element in nature, or a unique color. Pick something a bit unique or unexpected so that when it does appear, you'll be reminded that this is the Universe working with you.

Exercise. I don't even like putting this on the list because exercise is not my favorite practice, but it's super valuable and I do exercise regularly. What I find most interesting is this: Once I invested in my physical body with a regular workout, my spiritual body felt better too. I felt more centered in all areas of my life.

Now I approach exercise like my spiritual life: deliberately, compassionately, and practically. I build it around my schedule in a way that feels doable, and then I fire up the iPod with inspirational podcasts or audio books and use the time for spiritual study.

Laugh. Look for moments to crack up. Seek out people and things that make you giggle. See the absurdities in life, even (or especially) during the hard times. Scientists have often proved that laughter is healing and good for our hearts. It is the sound of the spirit.

IMPERFECT SPIRITUALITY

Now it's time to take the practices in this chapter and those scattered throughout the book and modify and shape and adapt them in a way that feels helpful and true and livable for you in your spiritual journey.

The practice of Imperfect Spirituality isn't about following the rules or doing what others say you should do, it's about being flexible and open enough to rediscover your authentic self. It's about noticing and acknowledging all of who you are—the flaws and talents, the abilities and limitations—and using it to live from a place of love and compassion, awareness, and joy.

You don't need to discard, fix, or hide from the pieces that are less than perfect. Notice them, see how they've served you, and give them thanks, or at least a bit of compassion. Then use your courage and creativity to live close to your values, to accept what is and create the beliefs that empower you to find meaning and sacredness in the moments of your life.

Go on now. Pull on those sweats and your favorite old T-shirt and go forward with awareness and curiosity. Connect to your spirit. Tap into your divine energy. Be all that you are, and know that that is enough. This is the practice of Imperfect Spirituality.

ONE PATH:
DELIBERATE PRACTICE

It is while in the car, during the hour-plus commute to work that Jason Marshall finds time for contemplation and sometimes prayer. His lunch break at the law firm where he works in Oklahoma City is long enough for a twenty-minute meditation or breathing practice. The other limited breaks in his day are often filled with the writing or study of spiritual principles and world religions.

For Jason, living a spiritual life is a deliberate act and it's a part of everything he does.

"I have no more time than anyone else," Jason says. He is married and the father of a two-and-a-half-year-old son. "It's just me. It's who I am. If it is an important part of your life, you make the time, you practice."

His daily practice, he says, has fostered the connection to his faith, but also helped him become more self-aware. Though he grew up in a fundamentally Christian household, Jason views God as a creative energetic force. And spirituality, he says, is a flexible, practical thing that eases his stress and helps him stay grounded.

"It's helped me to become comfortable with who I am instead of becoming who others think I should be. There's a confidence that comes with that. I don't feel like I need to fit a certain persona. I can be me."

That self-confidence helps him keep cool in the courtroom. When things turn adversarial, as is often the nature of lawsuits, Jason says he can still argue his case with a certain compassion or understanding. He doesn't take the conflict personally, nor does he feel anger at the opposing council. He is a spiritual being, not a man dependent on winning or losing.

But, like everyone, Jason has times when he snaps from fatigue or stress, where his actions come from his head, not his heart.

"You can be spiritual but you'll still be an imperfect human being. I try to catch myself. I apologize when I don't do it well. I think part of being a spiritual person is to be committed to learning and trying to live better. So, after those times, you have to dust yourself off and try your best not to repeat the mistakes. But you can do this compassionately. You don't have to beat yourself up."

After work, Jason tries to find a moment for a quick break on the back deck where he offers a prayer of thankfulness for the day.

"Spirituality can be simple," he says. "It shows up in all the small ways you live your life, in the time you take to say thanks."

"When I pray I don't rattle off a wish list of things I want. I think of it more about becoming aware and mindful of all that is already here. Of course once in a while you're interrupted by a noisy car passing by," he laughs, "but you do the best you can."

Chapter 13:

In the End, Beginning Again

Keep on beginning and failing. Each time you fail, start all over again, and you will grow stronger until you have accomplished a purpose—not the one you began with perhaps, but one you'll be glad to remember.

— ANNIE SULLIVAN

I t was dark by the time I finished writing the chapter called "Relating to the Imperfection in Others." Like so many things in this book, the themes in that chapter resonated with me and I was revved up on compassion and tolerance. Clear on how the flaws in our marriage and each other were really strengths. Accepting of how our differences provided avenues to intimacy and self-knowledge. I was full-on feeling the love.

I shut off the light in my home office and wandered out to the kitchen. There I saw my amazing husband, sitting serenely on the couch. Doing nothing. Nothing. At. All.

I flipped out.

There was no dinner being made, no table being set. No cat litter being cleaned, or laundry being folded. No bath being run for the kid. Nothing. In a split second, I dropped from my place of love and gratitude through a trapdoor into the tumultuous, tight-feeling, stressed-out mode of geez-I-have-to-do-everything-around-here.

It was as though I left my spiritual self on the side of a desert highway and began speeding recklessly toward Vegas. The shift in my emotions and behavior was so swift, so reactive and angry, that I startled even myself. Then I just felt deeply disappointed.

How could I know all that I know, and practice all that I do, and still be such a complete schmuck at times? After all these years of study why do I still get so triggered? How can I be so connected to spirit *and* still in touch with my overreactive teen self?

I live and practice so much of what I write about here in this book and I also screw it up in such gargantuan ways.

The disparity that sometimes lingers between my heart and my head is unnerving and irritating and makes me prone to emotional eating. I know firsthand the power of compassion and yet there are entire days when I seem void of kindness. I love deeply, but sometimes still allow anger and hurt to settle in. I am sometimes muddled and anxious and resisting rather than accepting and clear. It is so completely and utterly confusing and annoying that I can be connected to my spirit in one moment, and popping off from my Ego in the next.

Too often, I let my mind call the shots. I let it manage, control, overanalyze, worry, plan, react, and talk back.

We all do this. We let our brains boss us around when really life only works best if we allow our inner self, our spirit, to operate our brains. The brain is powerful, the Ego important. We can use them to learn, make decisions, and accomplish goals. When we source our minds from spirit, then we become energized by ideas, aware to the possibilities, open and able to live with love. Then the Ego and our brains work for us.

Life is not a top-down deal. It's an all-around-inside-out operation. Our intellectual functions, our choices, and our reactions can originate from our essence and filter up through our minds, infusing all those ideas with love and compassion. Then instead of flipping out when I noticed nothing had been done, I could have taken a breath, remembered who I am (a spiritual being), become aware and accepting of what was before me (my slacker husband), and asked for the help I needed to get dinner done.

There doesn't have to be any drama. I don't have to build up expectations or lash out when they aren't met. I don't have to disconnect from my spiritual self to make it in this reality that is filled with dirty dishes and bad television programming. I can be all that I am, imperfections aplenty, and still live a spiritual life. I can face challenges and still behave as a spiritual being.

This is what I came to know while writing this book. When I began the process, I thought I would, like so many authors, be giving birth to a finished publication. What happened though is that part of me was born out of this book. The things I learned, the people I met, the awareness I gained, helped me to grow up and into myself. It helped me to see who I really am in a way I hadn't noticed before. I know now I don't always have to get it right. Life isn't a puzzle to be figured out. It is an experience.

We won't always do it well. But we can be aware of what we're doing. My daily practice then is more about awareness than anything else. It's about catching myself when I'm triggered and getting curious about that. It's about sitting with my anger to gain clarity for a few minutes before reacting from my head instead of my heart, because, in that moment's pause, awareness moves in. Then you have a choice. The choice is a simple one. You act from spirit. Or you do not.

In any moment, any single moment, you can consciously choose love over anger, curiosity over confusion, courage over fear. You can laugh and love, no matter what your hair looks like or how much you have in your bank account. You can forgive yourself for your imperfections and let them remind you to be compassionate to others. You can learn what you don't know, and use it to serve others. You can live with faith during the hurting times and stay close to your values when buoyed by success. You can experience joy for no reason at all.

This is what it feels like when I'm living from spirit. This is where I want to be. And in the moments when I'm not, in the moments when I'm imperfect, in the moments when I'm operating more from my head than my heart, I know, if I pay attention, those imperfections can also lead me back to my source. From there I can start again. So can you. In the end, we can all begin again.

About the Author

Buddha probably never pulled a raisin out of a toddler's nose on his path toward enlightenment, but stuck raisins and other real-life moments have provided writer Polly Campbell plenty of opportunities for spiritual growth and self-improvement.

Campbell's articles on personal development topics and spiritual practices appear regularly in national publications and blogs, and she is also a professional speaker who inspires and energizes audiences with a blend of wit and wisdom.

She admits to practicing many of the things she writes and speaks about in her own quest to find more peace, happiness, and sometimes just socks that match, during her days as a multitasking wife and mother.

Campbell is also an avid player of Go Fish, a forever fan of the Oregon Ducks, and a reader of personal development and spirituality books. She lives in Oregon.

You can find her at www.imperfectspirituality.com.

Photograph by David Kinder/Kinderpics.